I. (Isaac) Hellmuth

The Divine Dispensations and their Gradual Development

I. (Isaac) Hellmuth

The Divine Dispensations and their Gradual Development

ISBN/EAN: 9783744660839

Printed in Europe, USA, Canada, Australia, Japan

Cover: Foto ©Thomas Meinert / pixelio.de

More available books at **www.hansebooks.com**

THE
DIVINE DISPENSATIONS

AND THEIR

GRADUAL DEVELOPMENT:

Eight Discourses

PREACHED IN HURON COLLEGE CHAPEL DURING MICHAELMAS TERM, 1865.

By J. HELLMUTH, D.D.,

ARCHDEACON OF HURON, PRINCIPAL AND DIVINITY PROFESSOR,
HURON COLLEGE, LONDON, CANADA WEST.

LONDON:
JAMES NISBET & CO., 21 BERNERS STREET.
TORONTO: JAMES CAMPBELL & SON, AND ROLLO & ADAM.
MONTREAL: JAMES CAMPBELL & SON.
MDCCCLXVI.

PREFATORY NOTE.

THE following course of Sermons was preached in Huron College Chapel during the present term, (Michaelmas 1865.) They were prepared in the midst of many engagements and college labours.

A desire, however, having been expressed by friends, whose opinion I value, that they should be published, I willingly yielded to their request.

My fervent prayer is, that the Holy

Spirit's influence may accompany the preached Word, and that this feeble effort *in defence of God's truth* may be owned and blessed of God, for the furtherance of His own glory, and the good of His Church.

Huron College, London, Canada West,
December 1865.

CONTENTS.

		PAGE
I.	INTRODUCTORY DISCOURSE—THE GRADUAL DEVELOPMENT OF THE DIVINE DISPENSATIONS,	1
II.	ON THE AUTHENTICITY AND GENUINENESS OF THE PENTATEUCH,	22
III.	THE TESTIMONY OF THE MOSAIC RECORD,	44
IV.	THE SELECTION OF THE JEWISH NATION FOR THE PRESERVATION OF THE KNOWLEDGE OF THE TRUE GOD,	64
V.	THE TYPICAL NATURE OF THE MOSAIC RITUAL,	86
VI.	THE TESTIMONY OF JESUS THE SPIRIT OF PROPHECY,	107
VII.	THE CONVERSION AND FINAL RESTORATION OF THE JEWS,	128
VIII.	THE CONVERSION AND FINAL RESTORATION OF THE JEWS—*continued*,	150

I.

INTRODUCTORY DISCOURSE—THE GRADUAL DEVELOPMENT OF THE DIVINE DISPENSATIONS.

EPH. iii. 10, 11.

"To the intent that now, unto the principalities and powers in heavenly places, might be known by the church the manifold wisdom of God, according to the eternal purpose which he purposed in Christ Jesus our Lord."

TO investigate the grounds upon which we build our confidence in the Scriptures, as containing a revelation from God, can never be a useless employment.

Even such whose faith is most firmly established, feel themselves sometimes disturbed by the unexpected assault of those who should be the defenders of the faith.

The great enemy of our souls is also continually seeking to surprise us in some unguarded moment; and, when he cannot persuade us to rebel against the acknowledged will of God, he will endeavour to insinuate doubts concerning the truth of revelation. Those doubts may not, indeed, prevail so far as to make us reject its testimony; yet they cannot fail, whilst they remain in the mind, to occasion great perplexity and uneasiness. It is, therefore, by no means unprofitable, even to established Christians, occasionally to review the reasons which they have to give of the hope that is in them.

We fear that many, who, in the present day, bear the name of Christians, are far from having considered the subject with the attention which it deserves. Born in a Christian country, and of parents professing that religion, they have been taught, from their infancy, to look upon the Bible as the word of God. But they have never seriously investigated the evidences by which it is proved to be so; nor have they any better reason to give for their believing, than that their ancestors believed before them.

I would, by no means, be understood to insinuate that, in order for a man to be convinced of the truth of Christianity, he must of necessity have studied a treatise on its evidences; much less is it to be supposed, that the conviction resulting from such study is all we are to understand by faith. Even illiterate persons may acquire a persuasion of the truth of Scripture, as satisfactory to themselves, and as powerful in its practical effects, as can be attained by the most profound theologian. For he who has experienced the power of divine grace in converting him from sin to holiness; he who has been brought to perceive the agreement between his own natural condition, and the account given in the Bible of the fallen state of man; he who has obtained a saving knowledge of the Lord Jesus Christ, as his Redeemer, and of the Holy Spirit, as his Sanctifier;—this man, believing "on the Son of God, hath the witness in himself," and has an evidence of the truth of Christianity which, though he may not be able to communicate to others, is abundantly satisfactory to himself, and is sufficient to fill him with all peace and joy in believing. Still, even to such persons, it must be highly desirable to know how they may answer the cavils of unbelievers, who unhappily, in this age of perverted reason, are to be found in every rank of society.

So extensively has the baneful poison of scepticism and rationalism been diffused of late, even throughout the mother country, where Christianity seems to shine with brighter lustre than in any other land, and that not only by professed infidels, but by those who unhappily hold posts of honour and emolument in the Church—that it is impossible for any person, who keeps up an intercourse with society, to be secure against hearing the truths of our holy religion attacked and ridiculed.

It becomes, therefore, the duty of every one professing the Christian name to make himself thoroughly acquainted with the proofs of that religion ; and more especially is this the duty of all those who are, and intend to be, ministers of the gospel.

There seems great reason to believe that the

attacks which have been made against the Scriptures, or portions of them, arise from an imperfect acquaintance with their contents, which these persons have never perhaps studied in a regular and connected manner, and much less in the original language. The same cause prevents numbers who are by no means to be ranked with unbelievers, from having just views of the *design* of revelation.

To benefit both these classes will be my humble aim in this, and in a few following discourses; and may the Holy Spirit's influence accompany and bless the preaching of the Word for Christ's sake.

It is not my present purpose to direct your attention to the subject, how much man stands in need of revelation; how suitable the doctrines of Scripture are to his condition and his wants; and how little they have the appearance of being the offspring of mere human reason; but my design is to enlarge upon the gradual progress of the divine dispensations, and to show that the truths of religion have been unfolded in such a manner as none but a Being of infinite wisdom and almighty power alone could have devised.

It is to this gradual development of the divine counsels that the apostle seems to refer in the words of the text, which hint at a plan of the sublimest nature, and such as could have been formed and executed by no finite agent. He represents the eternal and all-glorious God as having "created all things by Jesus Christ, to the intent that unto the principalities and powers in heavenly places, might be known by the church the manifold wisdom of God, according to the eternal purpose which he purposed in Christ Jesus our Lord."

The words here rendered "according to the eternal purpose," (κατὰ πρόθεςιν τῶν αἰώνων,) seem capable of being more accurately translated, "According to the predisposition of the ages;" and hence we are led to consider this world as a spacious theatre, formed for the manifestation of God's glorious attributes to every order of intelligent creatures. His dealings with the Church are represented as having reference to celestial, as well as terrestrial, beings; for, "to the principalities and powers in heavenly places" are to be made manifest "by the Church the manifold wisdom of God."

These are subjects which we are assured the angels desire to look into; and, therefore, they surely well deserve *our* attention, who are the parties immediately concerned in them.

The principalities and powers in heavenly places may meditate on these things with delight, because they afford a marvellous display of the perfections of that God, whom with the utmost affection and reverence they continually adore; and because they also make known His designs of mercy to a race which, though now degraded by sin, is destined to be made partaker of a glory, scarcely, if at all, inferior to their own. But surely they have a far stronger claim on *our* study, to whose immortal happiness they relate; surely *we* must justly be deemed inexcusable if we turn away from them with careless indifference.

I trust I shall have your serious attention proportioned to the importance and dignity of the subject.

My purpose is to trace the gradual development of that plan which infinite wisdom and goodness have formed for the recovery of fallen man. But, since it has pleased God to make known His designs on this subject through the peculiar instrumentality of one chosen nation, it will be to their history that I shall chiefly confine myself, by illustrating the testimony which, either willingly or unwillingly, the Jews bear to the religion of Christ.

To inquire why God did not see fit completely to communicate the plan of the Christian dispensation to the fallen ancestors of mankind, is presumptuous in beings who ought to consider the slightest intimations of mercy as far more than they deserve. Yet, since this is a degree of presumption to which the daring boldness of rationalism and scepticism has risen, it may not be improper to offer a few observations on the subject.

God has graciously adapted His communications to the understanding and capacities of those to whom they were made. The plan of salvation through the incarnation and expiatory sacrifice of the Son of God, must be acknowledged to be highly mysterious. Even in this advanced age of the world, and after so much preparatory instruction, many sincere Christians find a difficulty in fully comprehending it; and it is probable, that even those who enter most fully into the meaning of the Scripture declarations on the subject, are far from possessing the accurate views which they shall possess when they no longer see through a glass darkly, but are permitted face to face to contemplate their Redeemer. How much more difficult, then, must the comprehension of such a design have proved in the infancy of the human intellect, and to persons overwhelmed with guilt and confusion as our first parents were when standing before the presence of their offended Maker. Enough was it for them to know that He, though justly displeased by their transgression, had mercy yet in store, and, though He inflicted upon them a part of that punishment which their crime deserved, would nevertheless provide a method by which they might be delivered from its most fatal consequences.

Let us remember what was the condition of the first generations after the fall. Compelled to derive their subsistence from the cultivation of the earth, which had been visited with the curse of barrenness; forced to defend themselves from the inclemencies of the weather, and from the fierce attacks of animals now become hostile to them; and wholly unacquainted with the arts of civilised life, and having no means by which to defend and protect themselves,—they had little leisure for meditating on deeply mysterious subjects, and stood in need of *sensible* impressions in order to be duly affected with the divine presence and government. There is great reason to believe that the knowledge of God was kept up amongst them by some *visible manifestation* which He made to them of His glory, and that by immediate revelation He gradually afforded such fresh light as at various intervals He saw fit to bestow.

Had the whole scheme of Christianity been revealed in the earliest ages, and had the glorious work of redemption been then performed, there is great reason to believe that these sublime mysteries would soon have been involved in allegory and disguised by fiction, so that, after some generations had elapsed, scarcely any knowledge of the true religion would have been transmitted to posterity. That this conjecture is far from being unfounded, seems manifest from the gross corruption of primitive truth even amongst the wisest nations of the heathen world. Search the Roman, the Grecian, the Egyptian annals; peruse the writings of their poets and philosophers; and see how faint are the traces of those religious communications, which were made to *their* ancestors in common with those of the Jewish nation.

Instead, therefore, of repining against Providence for reserving the full manifestation of the gospel to a more enlightened age, an age in which knowledge of every kind was extensively diffused and carefully preserved, we ought to be thankful for the gradual revelation of His merciful designs, and for the powerful evidence which this very mode of communicating them affords.

This is another subject highly deserving our attention. Revelation must either be made immediately to every individual, or be communicated at some particular time or times, and to some particular persons, for the instruction of others. To the former plan many obvious objections might be urged; to the latter it becomes highly important that sufficient evidence should be afforded to carry conviction to every candid mind. Now, much of this evidence must of necessity have been withheld had the whole plan of redemption been made known immediately after the fall.

One powerful evidence which our religion possesses, is afforded by the miracles which attended its propagation. A miracle is an interruption of the ordinary course of nature, caused by a power which is manifestly superior to any with which we are acquainted. Without a knowledge, then, of the ordinary course of nature, it would be impossible to judge what is, and what is not, a violation of it; and such a knowledge can only be acquired by long experience, and attentive observation of the phenomena of the universe. It must be manifest, therefore, that sufficient knowledge could not have been possessed by the rude ancestors of mankind, for miracles performed in their presence to have been deemed a convincing proof of revelation.

From prophecy also, we in these latter ages derive very satisfactory evidence of the truth of the Scriptures, and of their divine inspiration. But the argument derived from prophecy acquires its force from *the fulfilment* of those events which had been foretold at a remote period. A very considerable time, therefore, must of necessity have elapsed before the validity of this argument could be entertained.

If this reasoning be allowed, we must confess that it would have been very difficult for us to have been satisfied of the reality of divine revelation, had it been vouchsafed at once to our first parents, and to their immediate offspring.

On this account, therefore, we may see reason to admire the wisdom of God in making Himself known to new created man by a visible appearance, and continuing to reveal His will by some immediate communication from Himself, until the human understanding had arrived at such a pitch of maturity as to be capable of judging of the authenticity of a revelation delivered by inspired messengers.

The period actually chosen for the full discovery of His gospel, was one in which the faculties of man had attained the utmost degree of cultivation; when arts and philosophy flourished; when imposture could scarcely escape detection; and when it was certain that anything professing to emanate from the Deity must of necessity provoke the most serious scrutiny. At that period also the world was fully peopled; one great empire had extended its influence and its language over a very large portion of the globe, and means had been provided for the rapid diffusion of divine truth to the most distant nations.

Another important reason for delaying the full discovery of the gospel, might be to render mankind more sensible of its value and importance. We know that sceptics have in all ages been ready to deny the necessity of revelation. They have asserted, that the intellect of man is abundantly capable of discovering all things necessary to his well-being, and that divine instruction is for him unnecessary. But the history of those ages which elapsed before the manifestation of the gospel, sufficiently confutes these arrogant pretensions.

We find men, who had carried arts and sciences to the utmost height, who had pushed the researches of philosophy to the furthest extent, and who yet were worshippers of "an unknown God;" we find these very men slaves of the most abject, the most degrading superstition. Then came a few poor fishermen and mechanics unfolding and preaching truths to mankind, which the sages of Egypt and of Greece had assiduously sought for in vain.

Thus it was, as the apostle Paul declares:—"After that in the wisdom of God the world by wisdom knew not God, it pleased God by the foolishness of preaching to save them that believe."

The despised disciples of Jesus, whom the

wise men of this world accounted fools and enthusiasts, were made the instruments of communicating the glad tidings of life and salvation to mankind.

But whilst I offer with diffidence suggestions like these, I would by no means presume to imagine, that I have pointed out the reasons which induced the great Sovereign of the universe to make known His glorious plan of redemption by gradual revelations and successive dispensations.

It is sufficient for us to perceive, that He *did* so make it known; and it will be our wisdom, as it is our duty, thankfully to accept the gospel scheme, and to profit by the instruction which He has been thus graciously pleased to afford. All that I have attempted has been to show that none has a right to complain of the lateness of the full revelation, and that there is great reason to believe that no time could have been more proper than that which was actually chosen for the purpose.

Yet, though I dare not undertake to explain the grounds of the divine proceeding, I shall not hesitate to derive from that proceeding arguments in favour of the truth of Scripture.

After a repeated perusal of the sacred volume, and a serious meditation on its contents, I know of nothing which strikes me more forcibly, than the wonderful harmony of its various parts, and the unity of design which seems to pervade the whole of it.

The restoration of fallen man from his state of guilt and condemnation, to the favour and to the image of God, seems to be the great object to which every page has reference. Had the Bible been written at once, and had its various parts been all composed by the same author, we need not have been surprised at the uniformity of design which we discover in it. But, since the several treatises of which it is composed were written by upwards of thirty different authors, and at intervals very remote from each other, during a period of not less than 1500 years, it is altogether impossible that there should have been any collusion between them, and that they could have followed any preconcerted plan of human formation.

B

How, then, can this unity of design be accounted for, but by ascribing it to Him, unto whom are known all His works from the beginning of the world, and "who at sundry times and in divers manners spake in time past unto the fathers by the prophets, and hath in these last days spoken unto us by His Son!"

The glorious plan which He had formed was at all times present to His mind; but He saw fit to make it known to man by progressive discoveries, first affording them, when overwhelmed with the darkness of guilt and condemnation, some faint gleams of hope, and then causing it to shine forth with gradually increasing brightness, until "the Sun of Righteousness arose" in perfect splendour, as the Saviour of the world.

To trace the gradual evolution of this eternal purpose of God—to point out the succession of the ages or dispensations which He had preordained—to show how the Church, and especially the Jewish Church, has been appointed to make known His manifold wisdom under all the various circumstances in which it has been placed,—such is the design which I have proposed to myself, and which I shall labour, through God's grace, to execute to the best of my ability.

I am sensible that these views are far from being recommended by the charms of novelty, and that they have been set forth with great ability by many who have treated of the evidences of divine revelation. But novelty is not my object; nor can it with propriety be the object of one who has to traverse a region which has already been so carefully explored.

The attacks of the rationalistic party, within the bosom of our own Church, have of late been so frequent, and have been carried on in so many different ways, that the friends of revelation have been excited to bring forward every argument in its defence; and they have exerted themselves successfully to refute all the cavils of their adversaries, and to prove that the fortress of our faith is erected on "the Rock of Ages," and is not to be shaken though assaulted with the utmost fury.

Instead, therefore, of attempting to employ new arguments, I shall content myself with displaying the solidity of those which we already possess. I shall invite you to walk about our Zion, to go round about her and tell the towers thereof. I shall entreat you to mark well her bulwarks, that you may be well convinced how much reason we have for our confidence, and how firm that foundation is on which the hope of the believing Christian is stayed.

The Scriptures, if rightly understood, carry within themselves sufficient evidence. The design with which they were composed is unspeakably glorious; the plan which they set before us is inexpressibly sublime. The more they are studied, the more reason shall we find to acknowledge their indisputable truth, and to adore the boundless wisdom and immeasurable goodness of their divine Author.

To Him who is the giver of all wisdom, do we now look up for divine guidance and blessing in the task which we have undertaken. And may I ask your fervent prayer, that God's Holy Spirit may be present with us, and cause this feeble effort of ours for the defence of Bible truth to redound to His glory, the good of His Church, and the well-being of immortal souls.

And now unto God and our Father, be glory for ever and ever. Amen.

II.

ON THE AUTHENTICITY AND GENUINENESS OF THE PENTATEUCH.

DEUT. xxxi. 24-26.

"And it came to pass, when Moses had made an end of writing the words of this law in a book, until they were finished, that Moses commanded the Levites, which bare the ark of the covenant of the Lord, saying, Take this book of the law, and put it in the side of the ark of the covenant of the Lord your God, that it may be there for a witness against thee."

THE survey which I have proposed to take of the divine dispensations for the recovery of fallen man, will unavoidably lead us to look back upon the first ages of the world. Of these we can find no satisfactory account, except in that volume which has been always ascribed to Moses the Jewish lawgiver. To his testimony we shall have frequent occasion to appeal; and it may, therefore, be important to set before you a summary view of the evidence by which the authority of his writings is supported.

The first point to be established is, that the five books called *the Pentateuch* were really written by Moses. In proof of this fact we have the uninterrupted testimony of the Jewish nation, from their origin even to the present time. Such a testimony is in all similar cases considered a sufficient evidence.

Whatsoever doubt there may be of particular circumstances recorded by Herodotus—though many of them are monstrous fables concerning the Egyptians—no person has ever doubted that he was the author of the works ascribed to him by the unanimous consent of all ages.

It is universally allowed, that the histories ascribed to Thucydides and Xenophon were written by the authors whose names they bear, and this is supported solely upon the authority of tradition! Why, then, should we doubt the tradition of the Jews concerning the books of Moses? That tradition is confirmed by the testimony of many heathen writers, who certainly had as good opportunities of judging as ourselves, and who agreed in quoting these books as having been written by the Jewish lawgiver.

Thus Diodorus Siculus says:—"Amongst the Jews, Moses represents that God who is called JAO as the author of his laws." The passage in Longinus in which he calls him, "A man of no ordinary character," is known to every student; as are the references which the historians Tacitus and Justin make to him. Eusebius, in his valuable book "De Preparatione Evangelicæ," cites several ancient authors, whose works have not reached our times, but whose testimony to Moses is very striking. We possess, however, a still stronger evidence that these books were written by Moses. They contain not only the history, but also the religious ritual and judicial ordinances of the Jewish nation, which are so closely interwoven with the narrative, that they are incapable of being separated from it.

The observation of the law, therefore, proves the authority of the lawgiver. The Jews could never have been persuaded to believe that the ceremonies of their worship, and the rules of their civil polity, had been prescribed by Moses, unless they had known them to be so.

Let the ordinances of their law be seriously examined, and they will be found such as no individuals, and still less a nation, could have been induced to receive unless enforced by the highest authority.

How painful was the rite of circumcision! How severe were the punishments denounced against those who profaned the Sabbath, or wilfully violated any other injunction of the moral or ceremonial law; how burdensome also and expensive were the sacrifices! Surely, had any person professing to speak in the name of Moses attempted to persuade the people to observe such a law, he would have been treated by them with scorn and abhorrence.

But it must be observed, that these books do not merely prescribe some particular ceremonies as ordained by Moses, and only occasionally observed; they record them as having been continued without intermission from the time that he ordained them. Can it then be imagined that, at some remote period after the death of Moses, an impostor could have persuaded the people, not only that they had always known, but that they had always observed this law—that their male children had universally been circumcised on the eighth day from their birth—that on the fourteenth day of the month Nisan, they had constantly slain and feasted on the Paschal Lamb in memory of their deliverance from Egypt—that fifty days after they regularly kept a feast in memory of the giving of the law from Mount Sinai—that every seventh year, at another feast, they had been accustomed to emancipate all their Hebrew bond-servants, and in a solemn assembly of the whole nation to read this law in the most public manner;—nay, that the original copy of the law written by the hand of Moses himself was preserved amongst them, deposited in a sacred chest together with some other things which had been laid up there as memorials of certain signal instances of divine interposition. Could it be possible, I say, for any man to believe these things if he had never heard of them until the moment that the impostor addressed him?

In the text we find a declaration that Moses wrote all the words of the law, by which, as might be proved by various circumstances, the whole of the preceding books is intended—and commanded the Levites to lay it up in the ark of the testimony, that it might be a witness against all who should in any future age dispute its authority. I am desirous to lay particular stress upon this point, because it affords a ready answer to those who, from a passage in the 2d Book of Chronicles, are disposed to raise an objection against the authority of the law of Moses.

In the 22d chapter of 2 Kings, and the 34th chapter of 2 Chronicles, we are told that Hilkiah, being commanded by King Josiah to repair the temple, "found a book of the law of the Lord given by Moses," and sent it to the king, who was much disturbed on reading it, and immediately took measures to reform those abuses which had grown up during the reigns of his predecessors. Now from this circumstance, some persons are disposed to argue, that the writings of Moses were at this time unknown among the Jews, and therefore might possibly have been forged about that period. The text, however, will assist us to explain this circumstance in a very different manner. It was not that the law of Moses had been wholly lost amongst the Jews, so that no copy of it remained except the one found in the temple; but only that the book there discovered was most probably the original autograph of Moses, which, according to his direction in the text, had been laid up in the side of the ark, and afterwards, during 'the idolatrous reigns which preceded that of Josiah, concealed in some place of greater security.

The Pentateuch itself had been long preserved by the ten tribes, who for three hundred and fifty years had formed a distinct kingdom from that of Judah, and would never have received this book from the subjects of it. Besides, had the law been till then unknown, how shall we account for the existence of the temple, the repair of which had led to the discovery of the book? How shall we account for the origin of the priesthood and sacrifices, and for all those religious institutions which these very books of Kings and Chronicles record? How could Josiah in so short a time have distributed a sufficient number of copies to make his people acquainted with the ceremonial of the Passover, which was so soon afterwards celebrated in the most solemn manner?

Surely they would have been disposed to resist the appointment of an ordinance like this, if they had until that moment been wholly strangers to it. We cannot, therefore, reasonably doubt, that, though the children of Israel had grossly failed in the observance of the laws ordained by the Pentateuch, they were nevertheless convinced of their divine authority, and of their having been delivered to them by the ministry of Moses.

Having thus, I trust, proved that he was the author of the Pentateuch, I shall endeavour to show the credibility of the history contained in it.

We will consider, in the first place, that part

of it which relates to the times preceding his own. Concerning these a little reflection must convince us, that it would have been impossible for him to deceive his readers. Consider how few generations are represented by him as having intervened between the creation of the world and his own time. There were but six persons, according to his statement, to communicate the tradition from Adam to himself. He represents Methuselah as having been during two hundred and forty-three years contemporary with Adam, and ninety-eight years with Shem. (The chronology of the Samaritan Pentateuch makes this yet more striking, so that Adam was contemporary with Noah.)

Again, Isaac was for fifty years contemporary with Shem, and for one hundred and twenty years with Jacob. Joseph also, the son of Jacob, was contemporary with Amram, the father of Moses. Now, it cannot be imagined that a tradition which passed through so few hands could be materially corrupted. It cannot be supposed but that all those who lived at the same time with Moses must have possessed a general knowledge of the events which he relates. These events were too remarkable not to have been the subjects of frequent conversation. The history of the creation; the selection of Abraham; the descent of the Israelites from him—all these were facts too remarkable to have been credited by those who had received no tradition concerning them from their forefathers. Had Moses intended to deceive, he would never have represented the lives of the Patriarchs as of so long duration, and *that* at a time when the ordinary term of human life was reduced nearly to the present standard. Let the manner also of his narrative be observed.

Of the ages which preceded the deluge he gives us but a brief account, relating such things only as tended to establish those important facts —the creation, the fall, and the promise of the Messiah; but in proportion as he comes nearer to his own time, his narrative becomes more particular, and he details facts which could easily have been disproved had they been false, and which cannot be acknowledged as true, without confessing the most signal interpositions of the Deity with respect to the Jewish nation. To specify no other particulars—the overthrow of Sodom and Gomorrah; the miraculous birth of Isaac; the signal preservation and elevation of Joseph—all these are facts which the Israelites never could have been persuaded by him to believe, had they not known them to be true, and which, if admitted to be true, must confirm the credibility of the whole narrative in which they are recorded. But if we see reason to admit the authenticity of the statements which Moses has left us of the events preceding his own time, how much more powerful are the reasons which induce us to believe his account of the transactions in which he was immediately concerned!

There are only two suppositions, which can be alleged to account for the general reception of these writings by the Jewish nation, if we deny the truth of the history contained in them. We must either suppose that Moses deceived the Israelites, or else, that they voluntarily joined in the imposture for the sake of exalting themselves in the eyes of other nations as the chosen people of God.

I shall first show that Moses did not deceive the Israelites. Let us consider what motive could induce him to make such an attempt. Was it the desire of power and dignity? Yet in what manner could he have had better hopes of securing these, than by continuing in the situation to which he had been raised by the humanity and partiality of Pharaoh's daughter? Brought up in the court of that powerful monarch, initiated into all the wisdom of the Egyptians, having every prospect to succeed to the highest dignities of that mighty kingdom—could ambition induce him to forsake all these advantages in order to share the fortunes of an enslaved and persecuted people, who were subjected to the most cruel oppression? Surely such a supposition is too improbable to obtain credit with any man who has studied human nature. But, admitting for the sake of argument, that he aspired to the glory of delivering his brethren from their bondage, and that he esteemed the honour of being accounted the restorer of their freedom to be more desirable than all the riches of Egyptian royalty, were the measures which he pursued such as were likely—considered merely as human proceedings—to effect his purpose? Would any man of common prudence, at a time when those whom he was anxious to deliver felt unwilling to support him, have ventured into the king's presence, and have demanded the liberation of his countrymen under the pretence of being divinely commissioned to require it? Would he not have conspired secretly rather than have thus prematurely avowed his pretensions? Would he have pretended to perform miracles of such a nature, that any imposition in them could not have escaped detection?

When he had by every means collected his people together and prepared them for departure, would he not have taken the readiest way to Canaan, instead of causing them to turn aside into a defile which did not lead them towards that country, and from which, should their enemies pursue them, they could not possibly escape, unless the Red Sea were miraculously divided to afford them a passage?

Having conducted them out of Egypt, would he have led them about in the wilderness, instead of marching hastily forward, so that the nations which they were to invade should have no notice of their intentions? Would he have detained them so long in that wilderness, that the whole generation which he led out of Egypt, as well as himself, should die there? If ambition influenced him, would he have taken no means for the establishment and perpetuation of his power? Would he have transferred the rule from his own sons to a person of another tribe and family? If he wished to have the honour of founding a new religion, would he have laid the basis of it in a priesthood, the continuance of which must depend entirely on the preservation of a family of one man, who had only four sons, of which two died almost as soon as the priesthood was established?

But it would take too much time to enumerate all the proofs, that Moses could not have intended to deceive the people. That he would not have been deceived himself, nor have acted under the influence of an enthusiastic spirit, is evident from the wisdom of his laws, and from the unwillingness with which he confesses himself to have accepted the divine commission. Neither could he, even had he been desirous of it, have deceived the people. The claim which he made to their attention was founded on an appeal to miracles; and those miracles were of such a nature that no man possessing eyes and understanding could have been deceived concerning them. Was it possible, for example, that Moses could persuade the Israelites that they had seen the rivers of the Egyptians changed into blood—their lands covered with frogs—their corn and cattle destroyed by hail and lightning —their whole country obscured by palpable darkness, whilst all the children of Israel had light in their dwellings, and that all these plagues were inflicted at his word? Could he have persuaded them to believe the destruction of all the first-born of Egypt in one night, if they had not witnessed it?—that they had passed through the Red Sea as on dry land, the waters standing as a wall on each side till they were gone over, and then immediately closing for the destruction of their enemies? Could he have made them believe that they had seen Mount Sinai encompassed with flames and smoke; that they had felt a tremendous earthquake, and had heard the law contained in the Ten Commandments delivered from the midst of the fire, with a noise so terrific that they unanimously besought God that they might no more hear His voice, but that He would thenceforth speak to them by a mediator? Are these miracles of such a nature that any craft, any combination of philosophical powers, could produce such a deception?

False miracles are generally wrought in secret, and are of short duration. But the miracles to which Moses appealed were wrought in the presence of 600,000 men, besides women and children, all of whom were immediately concerned and interested in the proceeding.

Many also of the miracles which he records were such as continued for years together; such were the pillars of cloud and of fire which regulated their marches and encampments; the water issuing from the rock which followed them; the manna on which they fed for forty years, and of which a specimen was preserved to all succeeding generations; the preservation also of their clothes from decay and of their feet from being swelled in their marches during the same period.

I appeal to any man of common sense, whether an impostor would have dared to call 600,000 men to attest a declaration of such facts if not one of them had taken place? It is evident that these are transactions of such a nature as to preclude the possibility of deception and imposture. As little foundation can there be for the opinion that the Israelites, though not imposed upon, yet conspired with Moses to deceive the world. So far from acting in concert with him, we find them continually murmuring and rebelling. No sooner did they encounter any difficulty than they immediately wished to return to Egypt. They accused Moses of deception in not having conducted them to the good land which he had promised, and complained bitterly that the honour of the priesthood was confined to one family; nay, not only did the rest of the nation rebel against him, but even Aaron and Miriam in one case opposed him. Surely these were not persons who would have acted in concert with Moses for the deception of mankind. But if, by any means, they could have been persuaded to conspire with him in such an attempt, would they have concurred in attesting a narrative like that contained in the Pentateuch?

Almost every page of it presents to us some account of their infidelity, their ingratitude, and their folly. Would a nation, anxious to advance its reputation, have acknowledged the truth of what is related concerning their worship of the golden calf? Would Aaron have suffered his name to be introduced in such a manner? Would the family of Korah have permitted Moses to embellish his narrative with a relation which brands them and their adherents with perpetual infamy? Could the Israelites have endured those perpetual reproaches with which he loads them, declaring that they were a stiffnecked people, that they had been rebellious against the Lord from the first day that he knew them, and that they would in succeeding ages continue to resist his law?

Let any man attentively read the 32d chapter of this book of Deuteronomy, in which Moses describes in such strong terms the folly and wickedness of the people, and predicts their future rebellions and miseries, with which they should in consequence be overwhelmed, and I will venture to say that to any candid mind the preservation of this portion of Scripture, and the testimonies which the Jews have in all ages borne to its authenticity, will be a convincing evidence of the divine mission of Moses.

Instead of imagining that the Israelites would have conspired to countenance the imposture of a man who, on this supposition, so cruelly insults them, we have only to wonder that they have not long since destroyed every copy of his book, in order that they might prevent the record of their acts from coming to the knowledge of mankind.

The same consideration strengthens the arguments which I have already used to prove that no other person than Moses could have been the author of these books.

That which the Israelites would not have borne from him, they certainly would not have borne from any other to whom they could not but be much less indebted. Never would they have consented that such disgraceful representations of their conduct should have been handed down to posterity; never would they have allowed so burdensome a ritual, and so severe a code of legislation, to be introduced amongst them.

Most astonishing is it, and worthy of particular attention, that amidst all the various circumstances in which the descendants of Israel have been placed, they have uniformly adhered to their law with the most persevering constancy. Though they were perpetually prone to idolatry, yet they never attempted to invalidate the authority of that law by which idolatry was forbidden. Though they neglected the precept which commanded that every seventh year the land should be left untilled, they never pretended to deny that such a precept had been given them.

Though a great variety of sects have sprung up among them, and different parties have at different times prevailed, the law of Moses has been always revered as the standard of doctrine and of duty. The Pharisees, who asserted the resurrection from the dead, and the Sadducees, who denied that resurrection, alike acknowledged the authority of Moses. The Samaritans, whose temple was on Mount Gerizim, as strongly asserted the divine inspiration of the Pentateuch as the Jews who worshipped on Mount Zion.

To this day, the whole nation adheres to it. All conspire to declare themselves the descendants of Abraham. All assert that Moses led their forefathers out of Egypt, and communicated the law which was given them from Sinai. All agree in looking forward to the coming of the Prophet, whom he assured them that God would raise up unto them like unto himself, and to whom he commanded them to hearken.

If, then, it be reasonable in any case to assent to historical testimony; if it be impossible that a whole nation could be deceived with respect to the plainest facts performed before their eyes; if men are naturally indisposed to preserve the record of their own disgrace, and to hold themselves up to the eyes of mankind as foolish and ungrateful—the Jews could never have been deceived by Moses, or any person writing in his name, nor could they have wilfully concurred in attesting the truth of an unfaithful narrative.

The books of Moses, therefore, have the indubitable characteristics of truth, and the information they give us concerning the origin and fall of man, and the divine proceedings with respect to him, are to be received as records of the utmost certainty.

Having thus established a basis on which to found my reasoning, I shall, in the ensuing discourses, endeavour to prove that the nation of which Moses was the lawgiver, was chosen by God as the instrument to make known His intentions of mercy in Christ Jesus, to the children of men.

Let us, therefore, with grateful adoration receive the Pentateuch as inspired of God, in which we have the record—by prophecy, vision, and type—of Christ, who gave Himself for us; to whom, with the Father and the Holy Ghost, be ascribed all honour, glory, might, majesty, and dominion, now and for ever. Amen.

III.

THE TESTIMONY OF THE MOSAIC RECORD.

Heb. i. 1, 2.

"God, who at sundry times and in divers manners spake in time past unto the fathers by the prophets, hath in these last days spoken unto us by His Son."

THE arguments which were brought forward in the last discourse were, I trust, sufficient to establish the authority of the books of Moses. I shall therefore, without scruple, adduce the testimony of those books with respect to the communications vouchsafed to mankind by the Deity in the first ages of the world. The words of the text seem to afford a very proper introduction to such a disquisition, because they manifestly intimate that, though the discoveries relative to religion differed as to the times and modes of their communication, they all had reference to that one great plan which has been fully revealed to us by the Son of God. We are here plainly told that the knowledge of divine things was not vouchsafed *at once:* "God spake *at sundry times.*" He made Himself known to our first parents before the fall, He afterwards gave them an intimation of the plan which He had in view for their recovery; to Enoch, Noah, and Abraham, he made successive discoveries of Himself and His intentions, until, at length, He selected a peculiar people, to whom He gave a written revelation, accompanied by a system of ceremonial institutions which we shall hereafter perceive to have had a typical signification. "*In divers manners,*" also, did He speak to them. Sometimes He assumed a visible appearance, and addressed them with an audible voice; sometimes He made known His will by dreams and visions; sometimes by secret inspirations. The types, to which I have alluded, may likewise be considered as another mode in which He spake to them, and were a standing revelation of His intentions.

In the prosecution of my design, I hope to point out the harmony of all these communications and their exact agreement with the gospel dispensation, for which they were intended to prepare the way. If these premises can be satisfactorily established, the inference will readily follow, that it was the same God, who thus "at sundry times and in divers manners spake in time past to the fathers by the prophets, that hath in these last days spoken to us by His Son."

Though the account which Moses has given us of the earliest ages is extremely concise, it sufficiently fulfils the purpose for which it appears to have been designed, that of showing the gradual unfolding of the divine intentions with respect to the human race. He tells us that man was originally created in the image and likeness of God—by which is evidently meant the resemblance of His moral perfections, —and that he was placed in a state of happiness. The duration of this state was to depend upon his observance or neglect of a positive injunction given him. Though this injunction was of the easiest and most reasonable nature, yet man was unhappily prevailed upon to disobey it. By that disobedience he drew down upon himself the divine displeasure; he deprived himself of his resemblance to the Deity; he not only forfeited the glorious privileges which he originally possessed, but also entailed on himself and his descendants mortality and ruin. This unhappy departure of man from a state of innocence gave rise to the Christian dispensation, of which an obscure hint was vouchsafed immediately after the fall. To this hint we must, in the first place, direct our attention.

It is unnecessary at this time to detail the particulars of the first transgression, or to vindicate its history from the objections of infidels, because this has been repeatedly done in the most satisfactory manner. All that is necessary is sufficiently expressed, and with this we ought to content ourselves. We are told that man was tempted to disobedience; that the tempter assumed the form of a serpent; and that upon that serpent, a sentence was pronounced of so remarkable a nature, that it could not fail to engage the most serious attention of those for whose instruction it was designed, (Gen. iii.)

Now the generality of interpreters have applied this sentence, not so much to the serpent, who was the agent employed by the tempter, as to the tempter himself. They have considered it not merely as foretelling a warfare between the human race and serpents, but as signifying that there should, in after times, spring up, from the seed of the woman, a person who should be the Head and Captain of a chosen generation, between which generation and the devil an unceasing contest should exist; and that this contest, producing in the first place some degree of injury to the Champion and His followers, should end in the complete destruction of the enemy of mankind, and in their deliverance from the state of ruin into which he had plunged them.

It must be acknowledged that this interpretation contains more than can be legitimately argued from the words themselves; yet a little reflection will convince us, that to expound these words in a merely literal sense, would be greatly to underrate their meaning. Consider the condition of our fallen ancestors at this awful moment. Behold them standing in the presence of their Judge, overwhelmed with confusion and terror! Could it afford them any consolation to be told that a mutual hatred should exist for ever between mankind and serpents; and that these reptiles should, in succeeding ages, occasionally bite the heels of men who should revenge themselves by crushing their heads?

Is it to be imagined that the mention of an incident comparatively so trifling could have been important to them, or that it could have encouraged the contrite offenders to cherish hopes of divine mercy? Yet that they should be thus encouraged was necessary, unless God designed to give them up to despair, and to deprive them of every incitement to repentance and renewed obedience.

If, however, we view the matter in the other light—if we consider the sentence pronounced upon the serpent as a mystical intimation of mercy to mankind, it will then appear both suited to the occasion, and worthy of the Divine Being. It must, therefore, have afforded our first parents no small satisfaction to hear that enemy condemned, and to be assured that one of their descendants should completely destroy his power. They might reasonably infer from this declaration, not only that they were not so conquered by their enemy as to be unable to maintain the contest with him, but also that they should in the end be completely victorious. They might even venture to hope that they should regain by victory all that they had lost by defeat; that as by the triumph of their enemy they had been deprived of righteousness, of paradise, and of immortality, so by his destruction they should obtain a restoration to a state of holiness, and to the blessings connected with it. That our first parents would have deduced such inferences as these from the sentence pronounced upon the serpent—had no additional light been afforded them—is more than I will venture to suppose; but that they did cherish expectations of this kind, and that further information was afforded them, seems capable of proof from the sequel of the history.

After the declaration made to Adam—"In

the sweat of thy face shalt thou eat bread till thou return to the ground, for out of it wast thou taken; for dust thou art, and unto dust shalt thou return"—the very first circumstance recorded is this: "And Adam called his wife's name Eve, because she was the mother of all living." Now, it is reasonable to suppose that, in so short a narrative, nothing is recorded which may not be regarded as a matter of considerable importance. The mention, therefore, of the new name which Adam now gave his wife, claims particular attention.

Whilst in a state of innocence he merely called her אשה, the feminine of איש, "man," to denote her formation out of his substance; but now, in this state of ruin and condemnation, at the very time that the sentence of mortality had been pronounced upon them both, he calls her חוה, "Eve," assigning this remarkable reason, that she was the mother of all living. But how at such a moment could he have been induced to use this language, had he been wholly destitute of hope? Might not the sad sentence pronounced upon them have more naturally induced him to represent her as the mother of *death*, on account of her having seduced him to sin, and having rendered him and his posterity mortal, rather than as the parent of *life*, because a race of mortal men were to spring from her? But if we consider him as discerning in some degree the design of that prophecy which foretold that her seed should bruise the serpent's head, we may readily infer that he called her "*the mother of all living*," because from her was to spring that glorious offspring who should be the restorer of life and immortality.

We find Eve, a short time afterwards, using language no less remarkable than that employed by her husband. She gave birth to Cain, and said:—"I have gotten a man from the Lord," (קניתי איש את יהוה) which ought to be rendered, according to the original, "I have acquired," or, "am in possession of the man, even Jehovah."

The Targum of Jonathan Ben Uzziel strongly confirms this interpretation. He thus paraphrases the passage:—"And Adam knew his wife, who desired the Angel: and she conceived and bare Cain, and said, I have obtained the man, (or a man,) the Angel, the Lord," a title by which the Jews always understood the Messiah.

The sanguine expectation of Eve led her to hope that the promise would be immediately fulfilled. She thought that the divine seed was already given, and that the victory over the infernal serpent was to be immediately obtained. Too fatally did the event disappoint her expectation. But though she erred with respect to the time when the prophecy was to be fulfilled, her error confirms the opinion that she understood to what it referred, and that she looked forward to the incarnation of Jehovah for the purpose of triumphing over her seducer.

When the character of Cain proved that he could not be the promised seed, Eve probably fixed her hopes on Abel; and when his death gave the first example of mortality, her faith did not fail, but prompted her to look upon her next son as the heir of better expectations. She therefore gave him the name of שת, which signifies "replaced," or "appointed," saying, "God hath appointed me another seed instead of Abel whom Cain slew."

The event proved, that though he was not the very Redeemer, yet he was the person from whom the Redeemer was to spring. He became the father also of a religious progeny, who were distinguished from the profane descendants of Cain, and who might be considered as the seed of the woman, in opposition to the offspring of that fratricide, whose descendants might not unjustly be called the seed of the serpent.

Amongst the descendants of Seth, we find Enoch particularly distinguished for his piety. It is recorded of him that he "walked with God," and his translation could not fail to convince his contemporaries that the sentence of mortality was capable of being superseded, and that rewards in a future state were provided for those who should exercise repentance, faith, and holy obedience in the present.

But the distinction between the families of Seth and of Cain did not endure for any considerable time. We find that they became blended together by intermarriages, and most disastrous consequences followed the unhappy union of the two families. It produced a deplorable corruption of manners:—"And God saw that the wickedness of man was great in the earth, and that every imagination of the thoughts of his heart was only evil continually; the earth also was corrupt before God, and the earth was filled with violence." Religion seemed to find no shelter amongst any of the children of Seth, with the exception of the descendants of Enoch.

We have every reason to believe that his son Methuselah followed his pious example, and we find in his grandson Lamech a remarkable instance of faith. We are told that he "begat a son, and called his name *Noah*, (נח) saying, This same shall comfort us concerning our work and toil of our hands, because of the ground which the Lord hath cursed." This language seems to imply, that he looked upon his son either as the promised seed, by whose means the curse denounced upon the earth for Adam's sin should be repealed, or at least as the person from whom that promised seed should descend. This proves not only that the original promise was in general well understood, but also that the expectation of its fulfilment was carefully preserved by the descendants of Adam.

Noah was likewise an eminent pattern of righteousness; and whilst all the rest of mankind was immersed in wickedness, he alone "was a just man, and perfect in his generation,"—he alone "walked with God."

In the days of Noah the great Lord of the universe would no longer bear with His rebellious creatures, but determined to involve the whole human race in one common catastrophe, except the family of this His faithful servant.

After the flood God was pleased to renew His covenant with Noah; the curse of barrenness seems to have been in some measure repealed, and an assurance was given that it should no more be renewed. The promised seed was also limited to the family of Shem, who was as eminent for piety as Ham was for profanity.

These two became again the leaders of two different parties in the world. The descendants of Ham soon plunged themselves into the grossest idolatry and wickedness, deifying the material powers of the heavens, and worshipping them with the basest and most indecent ceremonies.

In process of time the progeny of Shem seem likewise to have been infected with idolatry, and there is great reason to believe that the knowledge of true religion would have been completely lost, had not God been pleased to select and set apart one of Shem's descendants, by calling Abraham from his native country, and appointing him to be the father of a chosen people, and the ancestor of the promised Saviour.

Thus have we traced the gradual communication of religious knowledge from the fall of man to the selection of Abraham and his family.

Brief as is the account which Moses has given of these early transactions, it is sufficiently explicit to convince us that man from the earliest ages enjoyed the light of revelation, and was encouraged to look forward to the time when the incarnate God should retrieve the fatal effects of the fall, and should make complete reconciliation for the sins of the whole world.

The book of Job might perhaps be here referred to, as bearing testimony to this great truth.

That it is no fictitious narrative, but the history of a real personage who lived somewhat before the time of Moses, seems to be a fact decisively proved, notwithstanding the ingenious but unsolid arguments of the learned Warburton. In that book we find the plainest acknowledgments of the corrupt state of human nature, and the most distinct avowal of the expectation of a Redeemer who should stand at the latter day upon the earth, and be the restorer of life and immortality.

There is one subject, however, on which I think it necessary to offer some remarks before I conclude the present discourse. The universal practice of sacrifices from the earliest ages, corroborates in a very powerful manner the opinion, that the means by which human redemption should be effected were revealed to the fallen parents of mankind. Amongst the heathen writers we find none that can give any satisfactory reasons for this custom; yet, in all nations, it seems to have been looked upon as the best method of propitiating the Deity. In the new world, as well as in the old, this mode of worship prevailed. The sacrifices which were offered in Mexico and Peru, when those countries were first discovered, were no less bloody than those of the Greeks and Romans; and, however they might differ concerning the Deity worshipped, in this way of serving Him they all agreed, though there is no ground for supposing that they had any communication with each other. The history which we have now been reviewing, does not indeed *expressly* declare that sacrifices were, in the first instance, of divine appointment; but it gives us sufficient reason for concluding that they were so. In the first place, we find it said, that immediately after the fall our guilty ancestors were clothed by God himself with the skins of beasts. Now, when we consider that they had already provided themselves with a covering, and that the permission to feed upon animal food was not granted till after the flood, there seems no way of accounting for the slaying of these beasts, but by supposing that they were offered in sacrifice, and that the appointment of their skins for a covering was designed to typify the concealment of our guilt by the righteousness of the great ATONER.

Immediately afterwards, we read of the oblations brought by Cain and Abel; and find that the sacrifice which the latter made of an innocent animal was accepted by the Deity, whilst the offering of the fruits of the earth brought by the former was not approved. Whence arose this difference? Why did Abel presume to destroy one of the creatures of the Almighty, unless he were assured that he should please Him by doing so? We know that God does not accept offerings which spring from the mere fancy of the worshipper, and have no foundation in His appointment; and surely an offering of this kind was one that, *à priori*, no man could have thought likely to be acceptable. The apostle Paul tells us, that it was *faith* which made the sacrifice of Abel more acceptable than the offering of his brother, and calls that sacrifice πλείονα θυσίαν, a word evidently derived from θύω, to slay.

Now how could Abel offer in *faith*, if no *command* had been given to him? and to what could his faith have respect, but to the atonement one day to be made for sinners? The language of God himself to Cain seems to convey this idea: "If thou doest well, shalt thou not be accepted?" If thou art a righteous person, free from any stain of sin, thine own merits may gain favour for thee: "but, if thou doest not well"—which no man in his fallen state can do—" sin lieth at the door." The word rendered *sin* is חטא, which in other parts of Scripture signifies "a sin offering;" and the word rendered *lieth* is רבץ, which rather means *croucheth*, and which, it may be remarked, agrees in gender not with the word חטאת, but with the beast which should be offered.

Another remarkable circumstance is, that we find a distinction made between clean and unclean animals before the flood; which, as they were not used for food, can only be accounted for on the supposition that the clean were set apart for sacrifice, as they afterwards were by the law of Moses, and as appears to have been the case with Noah's sacrifice.

Should these reasons, however, not be deemed sufficient to prove that sacrifices were originally of divine appointment, the very early and constant use of them seems clearly to show, not only that it met with the divine approbation, but also that it arose from a right understanding of the prophecy contained in the sentence pronounced upon the serpent. The death of the victim might aptly typify *that bruising of the heel of the woman's seed*, the effect of which was to be *the crushing of the serpent's head*.

And, though the heathens did not retain a remembrance of the true origin of sacrifices, yet their forgetfulness in this respect is no more than took place with respect to various other religious institutions; the practice of which they retained, though they did not remember what had led them to adopt it. Amongst the true servants of God, right views of the subject seem evidently to have prevailed; and few as are the particulars related concerning them, there seems sufficient reason to conclude, that to the very first progenitors of mankind and their immediate descendants, enough was made known concerning the important doctrine of the atonement to revive their drooping spirits, and encourage them to look to their Creator as a God of mercy, as well as to hope that the time would come when they should be completely restored to His favour, and reinstated in those glorious privileges of which their sin had deprived them.

Happy, beyond measure, are we who now no longer see these things through the veil of typical institutions, but are blessed with the full revelation of our Redeemer.

Let us prize our advantages as we ought. Let us place our sole dependence on His atoning sacrifice; and, remembering with what a price we are ransomed, resolve from henceforth to glorify God with our body and with our spirit, which are God's; to whom, with the Son and the Holy Ghost, be ascribed all honour, glory, might, majesty, and dominion, now and for ever. Amen.

IV.

THE SELECTION OF THE JEWISH NATION FOR THE PRESERVATION OF THE KNOWLEDGE OF THE TRUE GOD.

EXOD. xix. 5, 6.

"Now therefore, if ye will obey my voice indeed, and keep my covenant, then ye shall be a peculiar treasure unto me above all people: for all the earth is mine. And ye shall be unto me a kingdom of priests, and an holy nation. These are the words which thou shalt speak unto the children of Israel."

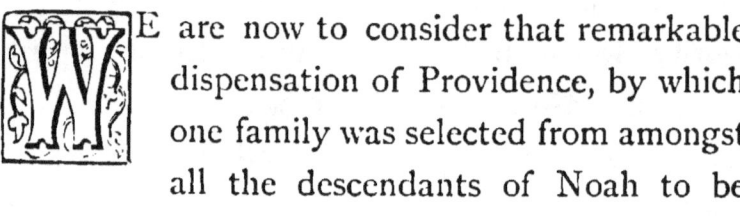E are now to consider that remarkable dispensation of Providence, by which one family was selected from amongst all the descendants of Noah to be intrusted with the divine oracles, and to be rendered instrumental in preserving the knowledge of the true God, and of His gracious purposes to mankind.

The selection of the Jewish nation has been

abused by infidels into a pretence for charging the divine proceedings with partiality. They represent it as an undue extension of favour to that nation, and as an act of injustice towards the rest of mankind,—so unreasonable and profane are the cavils, in which those will allow themselves to indulge who are possessed of an evil heart of unbelief.

Unreasonable, however, and profane as the objection is, it would not be proper to pass it by unnoticed. Let it be remarked, therefore, that the very persons who complain of the peculiar favour thus extended to the Jews, are the same who on other occasions assert that revelation is needless, and that the unassisted powers of man are abundantly equal to the discovery of those truths which respect his well-being both here and hereafter. Were this statement well founded, there surely could be no reason for the complaint which has been noticed; because, on this hypothesis, nothing was withheld from the Gentile nations which their own reason was not able to supply.

If revelation be unnecessary, the withholding

it from any particular persons can be no injury to them; if, on the contrary, it be acknowledged of such high importance, one of the main grounds on which our adversaries justify their rejection of the Scriptures is taken from them, and they must be compelled to confess that the existence of some revelation from God is a natural, if not a necessary consequence of His benevolence.

But the partiality complained of did not in reality exist. The essential truths of religion were from the first communicated to all mankind. We have seen how Adam was cheered by the promise of a Redeemer; and we are assured that the covenant, when renewed with Noah, was made known to all his children. Had their descendants persevered in obedience to the divine precepts, they would not have been excluded from the Church, or from the favour of God; but through their own wilful disobedience, they lost that knowledge of Him which they originally possessed. It was " because that when they knew God, they glorified Him not as God, neither were thankful; but became vain in their imaginations, and their foolish heart was darkened. Professing themselves to be wise they became fools. . . . And even as they did not like to retain God in their knowledge, God gave them up to a reprobate mind."

Such is the account which a Christian apostle gives of the origin of idolatry in the Gentile world.

Let the writings of their own historians and philosophers be studied, and the accuracy of the statement will be very manifest. They soon began to worship the material powers of the heavens in the place of their Omnipotent Creator.

They deified also their departed ancestors; and at length, uniting these two superstitions, adored the heroes and planets under the same titles, and with the same detestable and licentious service.

So rapid was this corruption of the true religion, that we may reasonably believe it would have extended throughout all the families of the earth, if one had not been chosen, and by signal interpositions of Providence prevented, from forgetting the true God, and from imitating the idolatrous practices of the succeeding nations.

The selection of one family, therefore; to be the depositary of the divine oracles, so far from being an injury, was in truth a benefit to the rest of mankind. I have already suggested some of the reasons, for which we may suppose that the advent of the Messiah was delayed till the maturity of the human race. Yet, though it might be advisable to delay that advent, it was nevertheless highly important that the knowledge of the divine intentions should be preserved until the period of their accomplishment arrived. The preservation of this knowledge was necessary for the consolation and instruction of those generations which were to precede the appointed era of human redemption : it was necessary also, in order that the correspondence between the prediction and the event might be fully manifest. If we sift the ancient traditions of the heathens from the fables with which they are intermingled; if we collect and arrange the scattered fragments, we may distinctly trace the expectation which prevailed among the ' Gentiles, concerning a great Deliverer who was to make His appearance amongst men. The notions, however, which they entertained on this subject were very imperfect; they had preserved nothing which could be considered as a direct prophecy concerning the Messiah's coming; nor could the identity of the person laying claim to that title be ascertained by comparing the features of his character with their ideas of it. Had the oracles of God, therefore, been left to float unprotected on the ocean of tradition, they would long since either have been dispersed in scattered fragments, or have been lost in the depths of oblivion; but, being collected into the ark of the Jewish Church, they were conveyed steadily along the stream of time, until they reached that period when their accomplishment in Him to whom they all had reference could be fully ascertained.

But it may be once more objected, admitting that it was right to select one particular nation for this important purpose, Why were the Israelites chosen? Were they not a people manifestly unworthy of the divine favour? Does not their own history represent them as in the highest degree ungrateful and rebellious? It does; but it at the same time declares that God did not choose them on account of their worthiness, nor on account of their importance amongst other nations:—"The Lord did not set His love upon you, nor choose you, because ye were more in number than any people; for ye were the fewest of all people. But because the Lord loved you, and because He would keep the oath which He sware unto your fathers." It is evident, therefore, that the cavils of sceptics on account of the unworthiness of the Jews falls to the ground. As far as any human agency had anything to do with the choice, it was the faithfulness of their forefathers, and especially of Abraham. He was, indeed, a memorable instance of piety. He was found faithful when his family were idolaters. He cast himself wholly on the providence of God, and in compliance with His direction forsook his kindred and his country. His faith triumphed over the greatest difficulties, so that he against hope believed in hope—"he staggered not at the promise of God through unbelief, but was strong in faith, giving glory to God; being fully persuaded that what He had promised, He was able to perform." When subjected to the severest trial which ever mortal man endured, he was still faithful, and was therefore rewarded by being made the father of many nations, and the ancestor of that Messiah in whom all the nations of the earth were to be blessed. The faithfulness of the ancestor may, therefore, in some measure (as far at least as human judgment is concerned) make up for the unworthiness of the progeny.

But let the nature of that unworthiness be well considered. What is there that can be alleged against the Jews, with which the Gentiles may not with equal force be charged? Did the Jews give way to idolatry?—so did the Egyptians and Chaldeans, the Phœnicians, and the Canaanites.

Though it must be confessed that the Jews were faulty, yet I may safely challenge those who are so forward in vilifying them, to produce any nation of antiquity which deserved a better character? Skilled as the Egyptians, and their colonists the Greeks, were in human wisdom and philosophy, did they excel in religious knowledge or in moral purity? Surely whoever will minutely investigate the history of these nations, as recorded by their own writers, will find that there was no superstition which they did not cherish; no vice, however odious in itself, and however debasing to human nature, in which they did not without shame indulge.

Since then, unworthy as the Jews were, no other nation can be found more worthy; since in selecting them God conferred a just reward on the faith and piety of their ancestors; since they were not chosen for their own sakes, but for the sake of conferring the most essential benefits on mankind in general, let presumptuous men no longer dare to arraign the conduct of Providence, nor to censure a dispensation which has been productive of unspeakable advantages to the whole human race.

Having thus, I trust, justified the selection of Abraham and his family, I shall endeavour to show that they were instrumental in preserving the light of divine truth, and in diffusing it amongst the surrounding nations.

The books of profane antiquity which have reached our time are so much more recent than the period now under consideration, that it is difficult to collect information on this subject from any except Jewish and Christian writers. But as some of these composed their works principally for the instruction of the heathens, and appealed to books which (though now lost) were in those days extant, we may safely employ their testimony for the illustration of those brief accounts which are given us in Scripture.

The Bible informs us that, after Abraham had continued for some time in Canaan, he was induced by a famine, which afflicted that country, to go down into Egypt. He was there rendered illustrious in the eyes of Pharaoh and his princes, by a remarkable interposition of the Deity in his favour. From thenceforth they treated him with the utmost deference, a deference which we cannot doubt that he would improve for the religious advantage of the people.

Josephus plainly tells us that he did so, and that he gave them much valuable instruction both with respect to human and divine knowledge.

Eusebius, in his "Præparatio Evangelicæ," cites many ancient writers, who give the same account of him, and represent him as a man of singular piety and wisdom.

The Persians long retained the memory of his excellence and instructions; and the Arabians, who were descended from him in the line of Ishmael, to this day venerate his name, and doubtless for a considerable time observed his precepts. That they did so we may infer from the singular piety of Job, as well as from that of Jethro the priest of Midian.

Maimonides tells us, that Abraham left a book behind him on the subject of instructing proselytes. At any rate, his zeal for the honour of God and the instruction of mankind must have produced the happiest effects for the time being. The same may be said to a certain extent of Isaac and Jacob.

In this salutary manner was the family of

Abraham employed to disseminate the knowledge of the true God, and to enter their solemn protest against idolatry throughout those extensive regions where learning and commerce peculiarly flourished, and from whence the knowledge of such memorable transactions could not fail to be very widely diffused.

But it was in Egypt especially that God was pleased to signalise His power, and to establish His pre-eminence over every other object of worship. For this purpose, by a wonderful series of providential dispensations, Joseph the son of Jacob was first carried into Egypt as a slave, and then exalted almost to the throne of Pharaoh, becoming a benefactor to that kingdom, and to all the lands surrounding. In this elevated station he appears to have continued till his death, which was about eighty years afterwards. During that interval, we may be assured that he employed his power, and exercised his rare abilities, in counteracting the progress of superstition and idolatry, and in promoting the knowledge of true religion.

By the benefits which Joseph was enabled to confer on the Egyptians, he not only gained a favourable reception for the dictates of a pure theology, but also provided a secure asylum for his family, until it had become strong enough to survive the oppressions which it was destined to sustain from the cruelty of this ungrateful nation.

It may not be improper to take notice in this place of the light which has been thrown upon the history of this period by the students of Oriental literature. It has always seemed difficult to explain the circumstance of Pharaoh's possessing sheep and employing shepherds, at a time when shepherds were an abomination to the Egyptians; nor has it failed to excite surprise that another king should so soon arise who knew not Joseph. The account also which Josephus, in his book against Apion, extracts from Manetho concerning the Hycsi or shepherd-kings, has occasioned no small perplexity to the learned. These difficulties are now removed by the Sanscrit writings.

It appears from thence, that Egypt and its

THE KNOWLEDGE OF THE TRUE GOD. 77

history were well known to the Hindoos, and that a tribe, called *the Palli*, emigrated from Hindostan, and established itself in Egypt. These Palli either left India before the doctrine concerning the transmigration of the soul into the bodies of inferior animals was propagated by Buddha, or else, as is highly probable, were expelled on account of their opposition to it. Like other shepherds, they fed on the flesh of sheep and goats, which the Egyptians reverenced as sacred animals, and the eating of which they consequently abhorred.

It seems, therefore, to have been by a signal interposition of Providence, that this Hindoo race was brought into Egypt, and possessed itself of the supreme power a little before the period that Joseph was brought into that country. After enjoying the pre-eminence for two hundred and fifty-nine years, they were expelled by a general insurrection of the native princes.

"It was," as a writer observes, "under this new dynasty of Egyptian kings,* who knew not Joseph, and to whom shepherds were an

---
* *i.e.*, The native princes who expelled the Palli.

abomination—an abomination not only because they reared cows, sheep, and goats (the gods of Egypt) for the purpose of feeding upon them; whereas fish, grain, and some kinds of birds formed the principal provision of the native Egyptians—but because the Phœnician shepherds were the conquerors of their country, and ruled them two centuries and a half with a rod of iron;—it was under this dynasty, I say, that the Israelites were so grievously oppressed, from a spirit of deep-rooted revenge in their new sovereigns and of jealousy of their increasing numbers; and it was also on one of the Pharaohs who constituted it that their Almighty Deliverer got Himself glory by involving the tyrant and his host in the waters of the Red Sea."*

Whoever will compare the whole of the statement given by this writer with the account which Josephus has preserved of the Hyesi or shepherd-kings, will see what a striking correspondence there is between them, and how remarkably they explain and corroborate each other; they will also, if attentively studied, be found to

* *Vide* Maurice's Hist. of Hindostan, vol. ii., part I, p. 203.

THE KNOWLEDGE OF THE TRUE GOD.

yield a strong confirmation to the narrative of Moses.

The ancient princes of Égypt having thus recovered the dominion of which they had been for a time deprived, revenged themselves on the children of Israel for the injuries which they had sustained from the former patrons of that chosen people, and returned to the idolatries from which they had probably been in a degree restrained. In those idolatries the Israelites seem to have been but too much disposed to join with their oppressors; and therefore God established in the fullest manner His superiority to the false deities of Egypt, whilst by the most signal displays of His power, He opened a way for His people's deliverance.

We must by no means consider the plagues, which Moses was commissioned to inflict on the Egyptians, as arbitrary exertions of Omnipotence. Several eminent writers have proved that each of these plagues was peculiarly adapted to the case of this people.

Their gods were made their tormentors, or were involved in like suffering with themselves;

and those things which their blind superstition regarded with peculiar veneration were rendered instrumental for their punishment. Their sacred river, in which they performed their ablutions, was changed into blood, which they regarded with the greatest horror;—its fish, esteemed sacred, also died, and filled the land with pestilential vapours. From the same river proceeded frogs, which defiled their land, and rendered their palaces and temples hateful. The affected delicacy and external purity which they observed in their persons (notwithstanding the detestable impurities practised in their temples) were assaulted by the plague of lice,—a plague that compelled even the magicians to acknowledge the finger of God. Then followed the grievous murrain, a judgment "very significant in its execution and purport. For, when the distemper spread irresistibly over the country, the Egyptians not only suffered a severe loss, but what was of far greater consequence, they saw the representations of their deities, and their deities themselves, sink before the God of the Hebrews."

On the other plagues the like observations may be made; not only did they afflict the hardened Egyptians with gradually-increasing severity, but also made the impotence of their idols more apparent.

Thus truly was the divine declaration fulfilled: "Against all the gods of Egypt I will execute judgment:" thus reasonable was the inference of Jethro—"Now I know that Jehovah is greater than all gods: for in the thing wherein they dealt proudly he was above them."

Subdued at length by these manifestations of the God of Israel, Pharaoh consented to their departure. But in a short time he repented having given this reluctant permission, and followed them with his princes, his chariots, and all his host.

The conduct pursued by Moses under the divine direction was such as no prudent general, nay, no man of sound understanding, would have adopted, except in consequence of such divine direction. Instead of leading the people by the nearest way to Canaan, he commanded them to turn and encamp in a narrow defile, where they

F

had an arm of the sea before them, inaccessible mountains on the one hand, and the Red Sea itself on the other. Whilst thus encamped Pharaoh overtook them, and then it became evident that God had brought the Israelites into this apparently ruinous situation for the purpose of making His triumph more incontestible, and of involving their adversaries in inevitable destruction.

The Red Sea was commanded to divide its waters in the midst, and to raise them as a wall on either hand, till the children of Israel were passed over. It obeyed the mandate of its Creator; it afforded a safe and easy passage to His people; and at His word it again closed its waters, and overwhelmed at once the chariots and the princes, and the host of Pharaoh.

Thus signally were the great leaders of idolatry discomfited; thus marvellously were the children of Israel employed, as soon as they became a nation, to set forth the praises, and to vindicate the honour of Jehovah. By His almighty hand they were conducted safely through the waste and howling wilderness; they were sustained by a miraculous supply of food when no natural means of obtaining it appeared, and were at length led in triumph to take possession of the promised land, whose inhabitants—as the behaviour of Rahab and the Gibeonites proves—were well acquainted with the mighty acts of the Lord, and, though unwilling to obey His laws, could not refrain from acknowledging His supreme dominion.

Their long abode in the wilderness, instead of being, as some daring infidels have pretended, a ground of objection to the conduct of Divine Providence, was admirably subservient to the design of their Almighty Sovereign. Had they been led immediately into Canaan, they might have been in great danger of lapsing into its idolatrous practices, which very much resembled those of the country they had left. This delay in the wilderness afforded time for the inhabitants of Canaan either to repent of and forsake their iniquities, or to fill up the measure of them, and thus become ripe for vengeance.

But what was of the utmost importance, it gave an opportunity of establishing such a system of religious ceremonies and of political ordinances as could not easily have been introduced, except whilst they were living together as one family, and had no concerns to occupy them but such as were of a religious nature. To this system of ritual observances, which was established during the abode of Israel in the wilderness, I propose to call your attention in the next discourse; in which I shall endeavour to give you some idea of their typical import, and to prove that by these the Jews were made God's witnesses with respect to those things which have since been more clearly revealed under the gospel dispensation.

Let us, my brethren, who enjoy full gospel light, admire and adore the infinite love of God, who, in His manifestations to the Church and to the world, gave a revelation of His will, clear and distinct—though "at sundry times and in divers manners"—concerning the salvation of mankind, and through a long series of years by the instrumentality of the Jewish nation—prepared the way for the introduction of His most blessed Son, who is over all, God blessed for ever.

And now unto God, and our Father, be glory for ever and ever. Amen.

V.

THE TYPICAL NATURE OF THE MOSAIC RITUAL.

Col. ii. 17.

"Which are a shadow of things to come; but the body is of Christ."

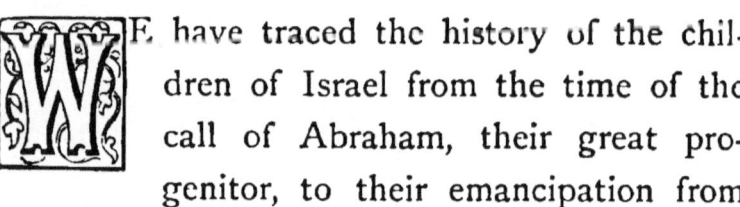E have traced the history of the children of Israel from the time of the call of Abraham, their great progenitor, to their emancipation from Egyptian bondage. Hitherto they had chiefly borne testimony to the true God by declaring those traditions which they had preserved uncorrupted concerning the revelations made by Him, and by worshipping Him in opposition to the imaginary deities of the heathens. But

being now assembled in the wilderness, and living together as one great family detached from every other nation, they received from God himself a law of ceremonial observances, which rendered them in an especial manner witnesses to the truth of the Christian dispensation.

It is of the utmost importance that the nature and design of this law should be well understood; because, whilst we are ignorant of it, we shall not only be unable to comprehend a very large portion of the Old Testament, but shall also find many passages in the New, exceedingly dark and unintelligible.

The apostle Paul found it often necessary to guard his Gentile converts against the errors of those false teachers, who maintained the necessity of uniting with a belief of the gospel an observance of the Mosaic ritual. It is on this subject that we find him reasoning in the chapter from which my text is taken. He exhorts the Colossians that "as they have received Christ Jesus the Lord, so they should walk in him;" that they should neither allow the pretended wise men of this world to "spoil them through philosophy and vain deceit," nor the Judaising teachers to entangle them in their traditions. He asserts, that by their baptism they were buried with Christ, and risen again through faith in His resurrection—wherefore they had no need of the outward circumcision of the flesh which had the same import; neither should they allow any man to judge them in meat or drink, nor in respect of an holy day, or of the new moon, or of the Sabbath days. For these, he says, "are a shadow of good things to come, but the body is of Christ."

We are not likely, my brethren, to fall into those errors against which St Paul wished to guard the Colossians; nevertheless, it may be profitable for us to meditate on the relation between the shadow and the substance; because such meditation may increase our conviction of the truth and excellence of our holy religion; may give us an insight into the typical nature of the Mosaic ritual, and may incite our gratitude for deliverance from the burdensome yoke of the ceremonial law, and for the enjoyment of the substantial blessings of the gospel.

When we consider with what minute exactness every particular relative to the tabernacle and its utensils was prescribed to Moses by God himself, who strictly charged him to make all things after the pattern which was showed him in the mount; when we remember that the workmen employed in their construction were specially inspired for the purpose; when we seriously study the directions given for the consecration of the priests, and for every part of their ministry,—we cannot but imagine that something more than can be learned from the bare letter was intended. This opinion is greatly strengthened by the recollection of David's earnestness in studying the divine law. What need was there for him to meditate on it day and night, if it contained nothing more than a description of ceremonies, which were obvious to the most superficial observer? Why should he have prayed so earnestly, "Open thou mine eyes, that I may behold wondrous things out of thy law," if he did not believe that truly wonderful and important lessons were to be derived from it? Surely the ardour of his inquiries must convince us that he looked beyond the letter to the spirit, and was able to pierce that veil which is represented as covering the face of Moses.

Viewed in any other way, the Jewish ritual seems wholly unintelligible and insignificant; but viewed according to the light which is thrown upon it by the writers of the New Testament, and especially by St Paul in his Epistle to the Hebrews, it appears a noble system, worthy of its Divine Author, and admirably calculated for the purpose which it was designed to answer. I would therefore invite you, brethren, to take such a survey as our time may permit of the principal features of this ritual. In doing which I would begin with the tabernacle, because the first directions given to Moses related to it and its furniture.

The first part was "the court of the tabernacle," mentioned Ex. xxvii. 9. This court was surrounded by a net-work, through which whatsoever was passing on inside might be seen by the people; and it seems probable that they were allowed access within it, at least, on particular occasions. Within this was the tabernacle, consisting of two parts, the one the holy place, into which the priests continually entered to perform the daily services; and the other, the holy of holies, into which none were allowed to enter except the high priest; and he only, on one particular day in the year, but even then not without the blood of the expiatory sacrifice, which he had offered, as well for himself, as for the errors of the people. Considering, then, the Jewish government as a theocracy, we here contemplate what we may perhaps venture to call the royal pavilion of the Deity, as we find Him saying to Moses: "Let them make me a sanctuary, that I may dwell among them." Here it was that they were to pay their devotions to Him, and here to receive those oracles which He was graciously pleased to deliver to them. But the explanations given us by St Paul teach us to enter more fully into the sense of these sacred symbols. The outer court seems to represent to us the visible church, into which all who profess the true religion gain admittance, but in which sincere and insincere professors are blended together. The boundaries of it would in this case indicate the separation of God's people from the unbelieving world, and from all who are strangers to the knowledge, the worship, and covenant of Jehovah.

From the outer court we proceed to the tabernacle, which, taken in its primary sense, denoted the habitation of the Lord with Israel; in its more special sense, however, it denoted the human nature of Christ, in whom dwelt all the fulness of the Godhead bodily. The outer part of this tabernacle was made of coarse materials, but the inner part of such as were highly valuable. So our blessed Lord—outwardly He appeared to be "without form or comeliness, and to have no beauty in Him that we should desire Him," though He was *in* Himself "the brightness of His Father's glory, and the express image of His person." The tabernacle also seems to have denoted the *spiritual* church of Christ, composed of His sincere and faithful worshippers, who are "an holy temple unto the Lord, and are built together for an habitation of God through the Spirit."

Lastly, we proceed to the *most holy place*, which St Paul expressly declares to have been a type of heaven, that sanctuary which is the special residence of the divine glory, as this was of the Shechinah, by which God condescended to make Himself at different times visible to mortals. Here were deposited the golden censer, and the ark of the covenant overlaid round about with gold, over which were the cherubims of glory overshadowing the mercy-seat.

Concerning these, though the apostle did not see fit at that time to speak particularly, he evidently intimates that much might be spoken. In a former chapter he had said,—"Seeing that we have a great High Priest that is passed into the heavens, . : . let us come boldly unto the throne of grace"—the ark therefore, of which the covering is always called the propitiatory or mercy-seat, was doubtless intended to represent that heavenly throne of grace, on which God is pleased to represent Himself as seated to hear the petitions of all who ask in His Son's name.

From the tabernacle we naturally turn our attention to him who was appointed to minister in it, and therefore may consider what was prefigured by the Aaronic priesthood.

It appeared that in the first ages of the world, the head of every family ministered in divine things before God, as we know was the case with Noah, Jacob, and Job. Afterwards the priestly office seems to have devolved upon the chief magistrate of the city or kingdom, as in the instance of Melchisedec, who was both king and priest; and in like manner Moses officiated previous to the consecration of Aaron. When the priesthood was established in his line, it was required that the priest should be of honourable and legitimate birth; that he should be free from bodily defects; and that he should cherish mental purity.

Let us consider how these things agree with our blessed Saviour. Even as to earthly parentage He was of the most honourable descent: of the line of Judah; of the family of David, and born of a pure virgin. But who can express the inherent dignity of His nature considered as the Son of God. He was indeed "holy, harmless, undefiled, separate from sinners, and made higher than the heavens." But as the Jewish high priest could not take upon him the office except as being called of God, no more did our blessed Saviour. He was chosen of a tribe different from that of Aaron, and made a priest, not after his order, but after the order of Melchisedec, whom St Paul abundantly proves to have been superior to Levi, and of course to all his descendants. And as the Jewish high priest was *consecrated*, so was the Lord Jesus. Aaron was first washed with water, and in like manner was our Lord baptized in the river Jordan. Aaron was anointed with oil, but Jesus with the Holy Spirit, and that in a pre-eminent degree, from whence He derived His characteristic name of Messiah or the Christ, which had from the earliest ages been appropriated to Him. The resemblance might be traced in many minute particulars, but it is necessary to hasten onwards to the consideration of the *manner* in which the priest's office was exercised.

This may be regarded as consisting of *three* parts:—The offering gifts and sacrifices for sins; the interceding for the people; and the pronouncing a solemn benediction on them. That part of the priestly office which relates to the offering gifts and sacrifices demands our chief attention.

The מנחה (Mincha) which our translators render *meat-offering*, (though flower and bread-offering would have been more accurate,) was of a eucharistic nature, and was never presented or accepted for the remission of sin, nor was any promise of forgiveness annexed to it, except when the offerer could not procure an animal sacrifice. The victims which were to be offered were to be free from every kind of blemish or defect; they were to be brought to the door of the tabernacle, and there slain to the honour of God; after which either a part, or the whole, was to be burnt upon the altar.

The *sin-offering* is described in the fourth

chapter of Leviticus. Its name (חטא) imports an atonement for sin. The person offering it was to lay his hand upon the head of the victim, thereby symbolically transferring his guilt to it ; and then, the whole sacrifice, skin and all, was to be carried without the camp and burnt, and its ashes were to be poured out into a clean place.

Here we see a striking type of our blessed Lord's death and burial. He was made to bear the sins of us all. He was offered up without the camp, and his body deposited in a clean place, a new tomb where never man before had been laid.

But the sacrifice offered by the high priest on the great day of atonement, was the one which in the most striking manner shadowed forth the death and resurrection of our Redeemer.

Clothed in the holy vestments, the high priest was on one solemn day in every year to take first a bullock, which was to be offered for himself and his family ; and then two goats, which he was to present before the door of the tabernacle. He was next to cast lots upon the goats, in order to determine which should be offered in sacrifice, and which should be the scapegoat to be set at liberty. After this he was to slay the bullock, carrying a portion of the blood within the veil of the sanctuary with sweet incense, which was to be burnt, so that the cloud of smoke should ascend before the mercy-seat whilst the blood was sprinkled upon and before it. There was he to kill the goat appointed for the sin-offering, which was for the people, and sprinkle its blood in like manner; making thus an atonement for the holy place, because of the uncleanness and transgressions of the children of Israel, and doing the same also for the tabernacle of the congregation.

By this offering he made an atonement both for his own household and for the whole nation.

Returning now into the *outer court*, he was to sanctify *the altar* by the mingled blood of the bullock and the goat, hallowing it from the uncleanness of the children of Israel. Having thus "made an end of reconciling the holy place, and the tabernacle of the congregation, and the altar, he was to lay both his hands upon the head of the live goat, and confess over him all the iniquities of the children of Israel, and all their transgressions in all their sins, putting them upon the head of the goat, and sending him away by the hand of a fit man into the wilderness—and thus the goat bore upon him all their iniquities unto a land not inhabited, and was let go in the wilderness." This part of the service ended, the priest changed his garments, and offered the usual burnt-offering; and the bodies of the bullock and the goat, which had been slain as sin-offerings, were to be carried forth without the camp, and burnt; both he who burnt them, and he who had carried the scapegoat into the wilderness, washing their flesh and their clothes before they were again admitted into the congregation.

This service is thus briefly explained by St Paul: —" Into the second (tabernacle) went the high priest alone once every year, not without blood, which he offered for himself, and for the errors of the people: the Holy Ghost this signifying, that the way into the holiest of all was not yet made manifest, while as the first tabernacle was yet standing : which was a figure for the time then present, in which were offered both gifts and sacrifices, that could not make him that did the service perfect, as pertaining to the conscience. But Christ being come an high priest of good things to come, by a greater and more perfect tabernacle, not made with hands, that is to say, not of this building; neither by the blood of goats and calves, but by his own blood, he entered in once into the holy place, having obtained eternal redemption for us." Again :— " Almost all things are by the law purged with blood ; and without shedding of blood is no remission. It was therefore necessary that the patterns of things in the heavens should be purified with these ; but the heavenly things themselves with better sacrifices than these. For Christ is not entered into the holy places made with hands, which are the figures of the true ; but into heaven itself, now to appear in the presence of God for us : nor yet that he should offer himself often, as the high priest entereth into the holy place every year with blood of others; (for then must he often have suffered since the foundation of the world:) but now once, in the end of the world, hath he appeared to put away sin by the sacrifice of himself. And as it is appointed unto men once to die, but after this the judgment; so Christ was once offered to bear the sins of many: and unto them that look for him shall he appear the second time without sin unto salvation."

Guided, then, by these instructive observations of the apostle, we may readily perceive, that the solemnities of the great day of atonement were a lively representation of the sacrifice of Christ for our redemption. He was at once both Priest and Sacrifice. The Jewish high priest, being himself a sinner, was obliged to offer for himself as well as for the people; but Christ made an atonement only for *our* guilt. Two goats were of necessity employed on this occasion, because it was designed to point Him out, both as dying for our sins and as risen again for our justification. The *one* represents *Christ crucified* making an atonement by His blood—the *other* represents Him bearing away our guilt, which was laid upon His head, and carrying it away that it should no more be remembered against us. The high priest entering into the holy place figured His ascension and entry into the highest heaven, there to appear in the presence of God for us. His return to bless the people, represents His second coming to receive His faithful servants to immortal glory. This leads me to mention two other parts of the priestly office which have not yet been considered.

As the public intercessor, when Aaron entered the sanctuary, he bore upon his breast and his shoulders the names of the children of Israel; so does Christ bear the names of His people in His heart and mentions them before God, in whose presence He ever liveth to make intercession for them. And as the high priest was authorised to pronounce a solemn blessing on the Jewish nation when assembled for public worship, so did Christ before His ascension solemnly bless His disciples; and so will He in a yet sublimer manner address all His faithful servants, when he cometh in His glory, saying, "Come, ye blessed of my Father, inherit the kingdom prepared for you from the foundation of the world."

Having seen that the Mosaic law offered a striking typical illustration of the means which God has ordained for the redemption of mankind, we have only to consider in what manner our purification from original sin was shadowed forth in it. That all mankind are born in sin, appears evidently to be taught by the remarkable law recorded in the twelfth chapter of Leviticus. It is there ordained, that, "If a woman have conceived seed, and have born a man child, then she shall be unclean seven days," &c. &c. In how lively a manner does this ordinance proclaim that all mankind are born in sin, depraved in nature, and stand in need of spiritual purification. But, besides the natural depravity of all men, there were many other cases of legal impurity described by Moses, any one of which, whilst it continued, excluded the person labouring under it from the privilege of joining in the worship of the congregation. The principal method of removing this pollution was by washing in pure water, which evidently symbolised the purifying influences of the Holy Spirit. This God intimated by His prophet Ezekiel, when He gave that reviving promise to Israel of the change which He will produce in their hearts at their final restoration :—"Then will I sprinkle clean water upon you, and ye shall be clean," &c. &c. "A new heart also will I give you, and a new spirit will I put within you; and I will take away the stony heart out of your flesh, and I will give you a heart of flesh." David also evidently alludes to the spiritual design of this ceremonial purification, when he says,—"Purge me with hyssop and I shall be clean; wash me, and I shall be whiter than snow," &c. &c. "Create in me a clean heart, O God, and renew a right spirit within me."

In this therefore, as in all the other ordinances, we see that the apostle truly said,—"These are a shadow of things to come, but the body is of Christ." We have taken but a brief and rapid glance at some of the ceremonies of the Mosaic ritual, yet enough to see that they shadowed forth the Christian dispensation. If time had permitted me to enter upon the subject of the passover and the other Jewish festivals, we should have been led to the same conclusion. But so far as we have been able to proceed, we may see abundant cause for thankfulness on account of our enjoyment of those substantial blessings which in these institutions were shadowed forth. We have Christ, who is the body of them all; in Him we are circumcised with the true spiritual circumcision. By Him, as the great High Priest over the house of God, we are introduced into the true sanctuary, that as a chosen generation, a royal priesthood, we may offer up spiritual sacrifices acceptable to God through Him. We have access into the holiest of all through His atoning sacrifice; we can draw nigh with confidence to the mercy-seat; we can consult the lively oracles which point out the path to holiness and heaven; we feed upon the bread of life—everything, in short, which is needful to give peace of conscience, confidence in the divine mercy, support in life, and hope in death, is freely imparted to us. Let us, then, be indeed thankful that the shadows are fled away, and the true light now shineth. Let us hold fast the head—even the Lord Jesus Christ. He is our great High Priest, who has entered on our behalf within the veil, and is thus for a short season concealed from us who are worshipping in the outer court of the sanctuary. But soon will He return, soon will He, who "was once offered to bear the sins of many, appear the second time unto them that look for Him without sin unto salvation." Then shall we, as many as thus look for Him, "appear with Him in glory." Let these considerations animate us patiently to bear up under present trials, which are designed to prepare us for the blissful portion reserved in heaven for us;—let us, girding up the loins of our mind, be sober, and hope to the end for the grace that is to be brought unto us at the revelation of Jesus Christ. Of which grace, may God of His infinite love and mercy make us all partakers, for His blessed and holy name's sake. Amen.

VI.

THE TESTIMONY OF JESUS THE SPIRIT OF PROPHECY.

REV. xix. 10.
"The testimony of Jesus is the spirit of prophecy."

THESE words occur in that very interesting part of the book of Revelation where St John, having seen in prophetic vision the downfall of the mystic Babylon, and the consequent exultation of the Church under the emblem of her marriage with Christ, declares that he fell down at the feet of the angel, by whom these glorious mysteries were disclosed, with an intent to worship him. This worship the angel repels, saying :—
"See thou do it not: I am thy fellow-servant,

and of thy brethren that have the testimony of Jesus: worship God; for the testimony of Jesus is the spirit of prophecy."

When we consider the manner in which this spirit of prophecy was dispensed, and in which its testimony was conveyed, we can scarcely fail to acknowledge that the hand of God was most signally displayed in it. We have already taken notice of some of the earlier intimations which He vouchsafed to particular persons concerning His designs of mercy through the Messiah. But we are now to survey a spectacle still more remarkable. We are to observe a whole nation selected for the preservation of the oracles of God—a succession of men during many centuries constantly predicting the same event — declaring that a glorious Personage should arise from among themselves, who should be the author of unspeakable blessings to mankind, and should establish a spiritual and eternal kingdom.

It was for this purpose especially that the Jewish nation was separated from all the families of the earth, that they might preserve uncorrupted the revelations which God was pleased to vouchsafe, and might bear an effectual and beneficial testimony to the rest of mankind.

It would be impossible, within the narrow limits of a sermon, to enumerate, and still more to investigate, all the predictions concerning the Messiah which are contained in the Jewish Scriptures. Nor is the task necessary; for they have been collected with the utmost assiduity, and their fulfilment demonstrated by many able writers. Yet that I may not leave my subject incomplete, and that our memory may be refreshed, I will briefly touch on some of those predictions, and refer such as are desirous of fuller information to the many valuable treatises on Christianity, especially to the dissertations of Bishop Newton on the Prophecies, and to Hengstenberg's Christology.

We have already seen how the promise of the Messiah, which was originally given to Adam, was further confirmed to Noah, and limited to the family of Shem. We have noticed likewise its restriction to the posterity of Abraham by his son Isaac, in whom he was assured that all the nations of the earth should be blessed.

Amongst the remarkable prophetic blessings which Jacob pronounced upon his children immediately before his death, we find the well-known prophecy which has always been understood to limit the descent of the Messiah to the family of Judah, as well as to mark the time of His appearance.

We find a remarkable passage in the fifth chapter of the first book of Chronicles, where the writer, in recounting the descendants of Reuben, observes parenthetically that "Judah prevailed above his brethren, and of him came the chief ruler." The original word for "ruler" is לנגיד, which the Septuagint renders ἡγούμενον, and both the Syriac and Arabic, "*the King Messiah.*" This seems to afford a convincing evidence that He was expected to be a descendant of that tribe. But the latter part of Jacob's prophecy is still more important, because it declares that "the sceptre should not depart from Judah, nor the lawgiver from between His feet, until Shiloh come, and that to Him should the gathering of the people be." That this passage was understood to refer to the Messiah is clear from various expositors. The Targum of Onkelos on this passage is very remarkable. He renders it :—" One having the principality shall not be taken away from the house of Judah, nor a scribe from his children's children for ever; until the Messiah shall come, whose is the kingdom, and to Him the people shall obey."

The prophecy of Balaam is another which well deserves to be considered, as it shows that even to the other nations some intelligence on this subject was communicated, and because it not improbably gave rise to the journey of the Magi, who followed the guidance of a star till they came to the lowly habitation of Jesus. The prediction of Moses concerning the future rise of a prophet like unto himself, has been shown by Eusebius in ancient, and by Bishop Newton and others in modern times, to correspond precisely and exclusively to the character and actions of our blessed Saviour; and this doubtless was the opinion of those Jews, who, after witnessing the miraculous supply of food provided by Him for the multitude in the wilderness, exclaimed: "This is of a truth that Prophet that should come into the world." The next limitation of the promised seed was to the family of David, who was himself an eminent type of Christ, and predicted many remarkable particulars concerning Him with the minutest exactness. The 22d and 69th Psalms mention many circumstances relative to His sufferings, which every careful reader of Scripture will be able immediately to apply; and we know that the words with which the former of these two psalms commences formed part of His dying exclamation. In the 40th Psalm we find Christ himself declaring that He would come, according to what had been written of Him, to fulfil the will of God by offering Himself instead of the legal sacrifices. Bishop Horne, in his commentary on this psalm, takes notice of an emendation of the original text which has been proposed, and which, by a scarcely perceptible alteration in the form of one word or two letters, brings it to the reading of the Septuagint and of St Paul, "a body hast thou prepared me." The 49th Psalm is a very remarkable one, and will be found by those who study it in the original to be full of gospel doctrine. The 7th, 8th, and 9th verses well deserve attention. After speaking of those who trust in their wealth and boast themselves in the multitude of their riches, the psalmist adds:—"None of them can by any means redeem his brother, nor give to God a ransom for him, (for the redemption of their soul is precious, and it ceaseth for ever,) that he should live for ever, and not see corruption." There is a very interesting comment on this by a Jewish doctor—Rabbi Moses Hadarsan—who says:—"This verse is spoken of the King Messiah, who shall die to redeem the fathers, and after that shall live for ever: He shall not see corruption." The gloss also of a Rabbinical work—Sephra and Midrash Tchillim—is worth taking notice of:—"A man shall not say my father was righteous, by his merit I shall escape or be delivered; Abraham delivered not his son Ishmael, and Jacob delivered not his brother Esau: he says a brother shall not redeem, &c. &c., to sig-

H

nify that no mere man shall redeem any." The 110th Psalm is acknowledged by the Jews themselves to relate to the Messiah. It was by a citation from this that our Lord perplexed the Pharisees when He asked them, "What think ye of Christ? whose son is he? They say unto him, The son of David. He saith unto them, How then doth David in spirit call him Lord, saying, The Lord saith unto my Lord, Sit thou on my right hand, till I make thine enemies thy footstool? If David then call him Lord, how is he his son?" This same psalm records the solemn oath by which Jehovah appointed His only-begotten Son to a far nobler priesthood than that of Aaron; it alludes to His sufferings under the image of His drinking of the brook in the way; but it enlarges more fully on His triumph, it foretells the complete subjugation of His enemies, and the establishment of His dominion over a willing people.

From the Psalms—many more of which might have been cited as referring evidently to Christ—we proceed to the prophet Isaiah, who has been justly called the Evangelical Prophet, on account of the particular delight which he seems to have felt in enlarging on the Messiah's advent, office, and kingdom.

His predictions concerning these are indeed interwoven with many which relate to the temporal condition of the Jews, and the nations with which they were connected. This was observable in the writings of all the prophets, and for obvious reasons. The covenant which God made with the children of Israel was of a twofold nature. One part of it was temporal and respected their continuance in possession of the land of Canaan and their enjoyment of national blessings, on condition of their abstinence from idolatry, and their obedience to the laws prescribed to them. The other part was spiritual and related to those far nobler benefits which were to be conferred on them, and on all mankind by the Messiah. Hence we often find an allusion to both these heads of promise in the same prediction, and in many instances we find spiritual blessings foretold by images which might at first sight seem to relate wholly to worldly advantages. The union of these two subjects had this important effect, that when the Jews found these predictions fulfilled, which related to events that were near at hand, they were the more disposed to credit those which related to a more distant period.

The celebrated Pascal observes, that the prophets intermingle national prophecies with those concerning Messiah, in order that these latter might not be without proof nor the former without advantage. These remarks may be exemplified in that memorable prediction, contained in the 7th chapter of this prophet.

When Ahaz, king of Judah, was under great anxiety lest his kingdom should be overthrown, and the house of David destroyed, Isaiah was sent and particularly directed to take his son Shear-jashub, who was then very young, in his hand, to assure Ahaz that within sixty-five years the Syrians should be conquered, and the Israelites carried away captive. He was also to declare that before the child Shear-jashub should know how to refuse the evil and choose the good— *i.e.*, should arrive to years of discretion—that the land should be forsaken of both her kings; or rather, as Bishop Lowth more correctly renders it: "The land should become desolate, by whose two kings he was distressed." So far the prophecy related to Ahaz, and the fears which he at that time entertained with respect to Israel and Syria. But in order both to confirm their hopes, and at the same time make this temporal deliverance the means of leading their thoughts forward to still higher blessings, the prophet, when Ahaz perversely refused to ask that sign which God commanded him to ask, took occasion to give the most glorious and comforting sign, not to the house of David only, but to the whole human race, by predicting the birth of Messiah, who had been so long since foretold to spring from that family. "The Lord himself shall give you a sign; Behold, a *virgin* shall conceive, and bear a son, and shall call his name Immanuel." Parallel with this prediction is that no less remarkable one of Jeremiah, (xxxi. 22 :)—"How long wilt thou go about, O thou backsliding daughter? for the Lord hath created a new thing in the earth, A woman shall compass a man." This Bishop Pearson has very satisfactorily proved, both from the literal meaning of the Hebrew words, and from the testimony of the ancient Jews themselves, to be incapable of any other than that obvious sense which Christian interpreters give to it.

In the 9th chapter of Isaiah, the Messiah is foretold, if possible yet more explicitly:—" Unto us a child is born, unto us a son is given : and the government shall be upon his shoulder : and his name shall be called Wonderful, Counsellor, the mighty God, the everlasting Father, the Prince of Peace,"—titles which manifestly belong to our blessed Lord, and which can be applied to no other. In the 40th chapter He is beautifully and justly described as feeding His flock like a shepherd ; gathering the lambs with His arms, and carrying them in His bosom, and gently leading those that are with young.

The 42d thus speaks of the satisfaction which He was to make to the divine justice :—" The Lord is well pleased for his righteousness' sake ; he will magnify the law and make it honourable."

The description given of His sufferings in the 53d chapter so exactly agrees with the facts of the gospel history, that there is no need of enlarging here upon it.

In the book of the prophet Micah we find a prediction which the chief priests and scribes, whom Herod consulted, applied to the Messiah, —"But thou, Beth-lehem Ephratah, though thou be little among the thousands of Judah, yet out of thee shall He come forth unto me that is to be ruler in Israel; whose goings forth have been from of old, from everlasting." That this prediction was very remarkably fulfilled—as far as related to the birth of Christ—is well known; for by a signal interposition of Providence the Virgin Mary was obliged to remove to Bethlehem from her own city Nazareth, at the very time that her delivery drew nigh.

The next prophecy to which I shall refer you is that of Zechariah, in which he describes the entry of the Messiah into Jerusalem thus: "Rejoice greatly, O daughter of Zion; shout, O daughter of Jerusalem: behold, thy King cometh unto thee: he is just, and having salvation; lowly, and riding upon an ass, and upon a colt the foal of an ass." It is not merely on account of the exact fulfilment of this in our Saviour's character and conduct that I have referred to it, but also that I may have the opportunity of noticing Bishop Sherlock's excellent illustration of it. In his fourth dissertation on prophecy he shows that God, in order to keep the children of Israel in a more implicit dependence on Himself as their King and Protector, forbade them the use of horses and chariots in war, and did not allow their princes to keep them; it was on this account the judges of Israel rode on asses, which are much finer animals in the East than those to which we are accustomed. David himself rode on a mule, and ordered Solomon to do so on his coronation day; and when the Jewish princes multiplied horses and chariots, they lost the protection of God and drew down ruin on their country. The Messiah, therefore, was not to be such a King as these, but one just and lowly, and bringing salvation with Him, not by the efforts of human power, but by the exercise of the strength of the Most High.

In conformity with this interpretation, the prophet proceeds to foretell—as others had done

—that the use of the horse, the chariot, and other warlike implements, should be cut off from Israel in the days of Messiah.

As the time of His coming drew nearer, the prophets spoke with increasing clearness. Thus Malachi in the name of God declares: "Behold, I will send my messenger, and he shall prepare the way before me: and the Lord, whom ye seek, shall suddenly come to his temple, even the messenger of the covenant, whom ye delight in: behold, he shall come, saith the Lord of hosts." Parallel with this is one, which I omitted to notice, in the 40th chapter of Isaiah, —"The voice of him that crieth in the wilderness, Prepare ye the way of the Lord, make straight in the desert a highway for our God."

Again, the prophet Haggai,—"Thus saith the Lord of hosts; Yet once, it is a little while, and I will shake the heavens, and the earth, and the sea, and the dry land; and I will shake all nations, and the Desire of all nations shall come: and I will fill this house with glory, saith the Lord of hosts. . . . The glory of this latter house shall be greater than of the former, saith the Lord of hosts; and in this place will I give peace, saith the Lord of hosts."

Having brought forward so many predictions which can fairly be applied to no other person than to Him whom we worship as the Author of our salvation, I will content myself with producing in addition only the one memorable prophecy contained in the address of the angel Gabriel to Daniel, in answer to the prayers which he had offered for the deliverance of his people from their captivity:—"Seventy weeks are determined upon thy people, and upon thy holy city, to finish the transgression, and to make an end of sins, and to make reconciliation for iniquity, and to bring in everlasting righteousness, and to seal up the vision and prophecy, and to anoint the Most Holy. Know therefore and understand, that from the going forth of the commandment to restore and to build Jerusalem unto the Messiah the Prince shall be seven weeks, and threescore and two weeks: the street shall be built again, and the wall, even in troublous times. And after threescore and two weeks shall Messiah be cut off, but not for himself: and the people of the prince that shall come shall destroy the city and the sanctuary; and the end thereof shall be with a flood, and unto the end of the war desolations are determined. And he shall confirm the covenant with many for one week: and in the midst of the week he shall cause the sacrifice and the oblation to cease, and for the overspreading of abominations he shall make it desolate, even until the consummation, and that determined shall be poured upon the desolate."

It would not at this time be in my power to enter into a discussion of the various explanations which have been given of this important prophecy. That which has been most generally received, is the one of the learned Dr Prideaux.

Like Sir Isaac Newton, he calculates the beginning of the seventy weeks from the commission granted by Ezra in the *seventh* year of Artaxerxes Longimanus, king of Persia, which was in the month Nisan in the year of the Julian period 4256. Reckoning from that period seventy weeks of years (equal to 490 years) we arrive at the year of the Julian period 4746, in the very same month of which, namely Nisan, our blessed Lord offered Himself up on the cross as an atoning sacrifice for the sins of the world. Thus far Dr Prideaux and Sir Isaac Newton agree. The latter, however, considers the seven weeks next mentioned as relating to a period yet future, and which shall take place at the return of the Jews from their present dispersion. He also calculates the sixty-two weeks from the twentieth year of the same Artaxerxes, and makes them end in the very year of our Lord's death. Dr Prideaux, however, considers the angel as dividing the seventy years into three periods :—1. From the commission given to Ezra to the establishment of the civil and ecclesiastical polity of the Jews, *seven* weeks or forty-nine years. 2. From thence to the time when John the Baptist opened the gospel dispensation, sixty-two weeks, or 434 years. 3. From thence to the death of Christ one week or seven years, making on the whole 490 years.

I am aware that considerable difficulties attend all the explanations which have been given of this prophecy; yet they are such as by no means affect the main argument derived from it: for it plainly determines the time of the Messiah's coming to a period, which every exposition agrees in placing very near that in which Jesus actually did come, and was cut off. It plainly asserts that this event shall take place before the destruction of the Jewish polity, as we know it did, and therefore it furnishes us with an unanswerable argument against the Jews, who deny that the Messiah has yet made His appearance in the world.

Even in the rapid survey which we have taken of some amongst the many prophecies relative to the Messiah, we must have seen that the Jewish nation have been made witnesses to a glorious personage, who was from the earliest period foretold as the Redeemer of mankind, and that the testimony contained in their sacred writings manifestly refers to Him whom we acknowledge as the Christ, the Saviour of the world. We find that the whole train of prophets which arose in this favoured nation foretold with gradually increasing clearness the advent of the Messiah, and related particulars minutely descriptive of Jesus of Nazareth. There cannot be the slightest ground for supposing that these prophecies were interpolated to suit His character, for the greater part of these were written before and during the Babylonish captivity, after which they were collected by Ezra into the sacred canon. The last prophet Malachi—as the Jews admit—wrote about four hundred years B.C. About three hundred years before Christ, the Septuagint translation was made, which prevented all possibility of interpolation, and caused the knowledge of God's gracious intentions to be widely diffused throughout all the civilised nations of the heathen world. After this period, we find such frequent allusions to the Jewish Scriptures amongst the Greek and Roman writers as prove that they had excited considerable attention. Virgil seems to have studied them with peculiar diligence, and in one poem almost literally copies the language of Isaiah. The result was a universal expectation of the Messiah's coming, an expectation to which Suetonius, Tacitus, and others bear an unsuspected witness

—an expectation which, doubtless, prepared mankind in no inconsiderable degree for the reception of the gospel, when it pleased God that it should be preached unto them. Contemplating this wonderful and harmonious arrangement of prophecy, it seems impossible not to be struck with the glorious display of the Divine wisdom and goodness which it affords. One ray of light broke forth after another upon a world which sin had overwhelmed with darkness and with sorrow, till at length "the Sun of Righteousness" appeared, and life and immortality were fully brought to light by the gospel.

May He, who has vouchsafed thus graciously to make known to us His designs of mercy, incline our hearts, by the teaching and influence of the Holy Spirit, to embrace His offers, and to hold fast the profession of our faith without wavering, for the sake of His beloved Son our Saviour Jesus Christ, to whom, with the Father and the Holy Spirit, be glory and majesty, dominion and power, both now and ever. Amen.

VII.

THE CONVERSION AND FINAL RESTORATION OF THE JEWS.

HOSEA iii. 4.

"For the children of Israel shall abide many days without a king, and without a prince, and without a sacrifice, and without an image, and without an ephod, and without teraphim."

HAVE endeavoured in the foregoing discourses to show how remarkably the Jews were employed to bear witness to the Messiah until the time of His appearance in the world. The spectacle which we are now to contemplate may at first sight appear totally inconsistent with that which we have hitherto surveyed. We are to behold the Jews rejecting that very Messiah, whose com-

ing they had so eagerly anticipated, and as a punishment, they themselves are rejected, for the present at least, from being the chosen people of God.

A superficial observer might be tempted to imagine that the refusal of the Jews to acknowledge the divine mission of Jesus affords a presumptive argument against it. He might at least consider it as unaccountable, that they who had been favoured with such remarkable predictions concerning the Messiah, and who had, above all other nations, been accustomed to desire His advent, should, when that advent took place, be allowed to harden themselves in unbelief. I trust, however, that it will not be a very arduous task to show that these events were foreseen in the divine counsels, and formed a part of the great scheme of Providence respecting the kingdom of Christ, and the salvation of mankind.

In order to understand the circumstances which led to the rejection of Jesus by the Jewish nation, we must look back upon the state of that nation at the time of His first coming.

Before the Babylonish captivity, the Jews had

been remarkably prone to idolatry; but when they returned from it, they fell into errors of a different nature. They adhered, indeed, with considerable steadfastness to the worship of the true God, but they allowed that worship to degenerate into mere formality. They laid great stress upon the external and ceremonial part of their religion, they overlooked and neglected the spirit of the divine precepts, and substituted an ostentatious observance of traditional customs, in place of taking the Word of God alone for their guidance in the path which leads to true holiness and life.

Pride and luxury advanced with rapid strides amongst them. The priesthood became corrupt and licentious. The people were split into a great variety of sects and parties, the most prominent of whom were the Pharisees, the Sadducees, and the Essenes. The great body of the people, given up to worldly principles, seemed in every respect to have lost sight of spiritual life and light. They had not, however, relinquished their hope of a Messiah. They were, on the contrary, aware that the period marked out by their prophets must be near at hand, and they eagerly expected His appearance, imagining that He would deliver them from the Roman yoke, under which they groaned, and would exalt their nation to the summit of temporal grandeur, erecting His throne above that of Augustus, and making all the princes of the earth His tributaries.

Possessed as they were with these lofty expectations, they could not in the meek and lowly Jesus recognise the Messiah, though He bore all the characteristics described in the prophetic writings; besides, the maxims which He inculcated were the reverse of those by which they were governed.

Instead of asserting His pretensions to royalty, and calling upon His countrymen to burst their fetters and to cast away the yoke which galled them, He invited them to become the subjects of a spiritual and heavenly kingdom. He promised them deliverance, indeed, but it was deliverance from sin. He offered them succour against their enemies, but they were the enemies of their souls. He loudly reproved their teachers

He set at naught those traditions by which they had made the commandments of God of none effect. He insisted upon inward sanctity as preferable to outward ceremonies. He also gave them to understand that the day was at hand when all the nations of the earth should be admitted to a participation of all the privileges which they had so long enjoyed exclusively.

Doctrines such as these were little calculated to gain acceptance with the great body of the Jewish nation. There were, indeed, some who waited for the consolation of Israel; but of the multitudes who flocked around Him to hear His instructions, to witness His miracles, and to partake of His benefits, only a small number continued steadily attached to Him, and not one had the courage to stand forward and vindicate His innocence when He was arraigned before the Jewish Sanhedrim.

The populace, indeed, retained almost to the end the expectation that He would assume the regal character; they considered this expectation as confirmed by His solemn entry into Jerusalem, after having in the most signal manner raised a dead man from the grave, and they therefore hailed His approach to the holy city with loud acclamations of "Hosanna to the Son of David; Blessed is he that cometh in the name of the Lord. Hosanna in the highest." But when, a few days afterwards, they saw Him bound by the command of their high priest and rulers, and dragged as a criminal before the Roman governor, their hopes of deliverance by His means were wholly at an end—they allowed themselves to be persuaded that He was an impostor; and they who had so lately rent the air with acclamations in His praise, exclaimed with no less vehemence, "Crucify him, crucify him."

Such was the reception which the Son of God experienced when, after being so long expected, He made His appearance in the world. Instead of receiving the honours due to His transcendent dignity, He was treated with insult and reproach; He was sold for the price of the meanest slave; He was made an object of derision to the lowest of the people; His back was torn with scourges, His face was defiled with spitting; He was crucified as a common malefactor,

He expired in ignominy and anguish. Thus low did *He* who was to be the Saviour of mankind stoop. But here His humiliation ended. Within three days, according to His own prediction, He burst the bonds of death and rose in triumph from the grave. He abode forty days upon earth, for the purpose of reviving the hopes of His disciples by convincing them of the reality of His resurrection, and making them more fully acquainted with the mysteries of His kingdom. He then, in the presence of them all, ascended into heaven with power and great glory, angels attending to show reverence to their sovereign, and announcing His second appearance to call the nations of the earth to judgment.

From this period a new dispensation commenced. On the day of Pentecost, which was ten days after, the Holy Spirit miraculously descended on the Church, and especially on the apostles, endowing them with many supernatural gifts, especially with the power of speaking divers languages, and enabling them to preach the gospel with such a divine energy that thousands were by one address converted to the Christian faith. The great body of the nation, however, continued in unbelief; and though they were urged with the prophecies of their own Scriptures which had been manifestly fulfilled in Jesus, and though they witnessed the most evident displays of the divine power, they still persevered in their unbelief, till at last God gave them up to the fury of the Romans. The lofty ramparts in which they trusted were not levelled to the ground till they had suffered a siege during which the utmost miseries from pestilence and famine prevailed. Their glorious temple was destroyed by fire; their priests were slain by the sword; myriads fell victims to calamities of every description, and the remnant were either sold as slaves or scattered as exiles and fugitives over the face of the whole earth.

We will now, with humility and reverence, inquire in what manner these events are to be accounted for.

The rejection of the Messiah by the Jews, though apparently contrary to the purpose for which they were selected, (*i.e.*, of bearing witness to Him) was yet foreseen and provided for in the divine counsels. Thus we find the apostles in their prayer acknowledging, "Of a truth against thy holy child Jesus, whom thou hast anointed, both Herod, and Pontius Pilate, with the Gentiles, and the people of Israel, were gathered together, for to do whatsoever thy hand and thy counsel determined before to be done." This acknowledgment they built on that prophetic declaration in the 2d Psalm,— "The kings of the earth set themselves, and the rulers take counsel together, against the Lord, and against his Anointed," (משיח.)

Many other passages might be selected out of the Psalms to the same effect. I will, however, content myself with a few quotations from the prophet Isaiah. In chap. viii. 13, 14, he says: "Sanctify the Lord of hosts himself; and let him be your fear, and let him be your dread. And he shall be for a sanctuary; but for a stone of stumbling and for a rock of offence to both the houses of Israel." In chap. xlix. 5–8, it is written: "And now, saith the Lord that formed me from the womb to be his servant, to bring Jacob again to him, Though Israel be not gathered, yet shall I be glorious in the eyes of the Lord, and my God shall be my strength. And he said, It is a light thing that thou shouldest be my servant to raise up the tribes of Jacob, and to restore the preserved of Israel: I will also give thee for a light to the Gentiles, that thou mayest be my salvation unto the end of the earth. Thus saith the Lord, the Redeemer of Israel, and his Holy One, to him whom man despiseth, to him whom the nation abhorreth, to a servant of rulers, Kings shall see and arise, princes also shall worship, because of the Lord that is faithful, and the Holy One of Israel, and he shall choose thee. Thus saith the Lord, In an acceptable time have I heard thee, and in a day of salvation have I helped thee: and I will preserve thee, and give thee for a covenant of the people, to establish the earth, to cause to inherit the desolate heritages." And again, in chap. l. 5, 6: "The Lord God hath opened mine ear, and I was not rebellious, neither turned away back. I gave my back to the smiters, and my cheeks to them that plucked off the hair: I hid not my face from shame and spitting." And in chap. liii. 1–3: "Who hath believed our report? and to whom is the arm of the Lord revealed? For he shall grow up before him as a tender plant, and as a root out of a dry ground: he hath no form nor comeliness; and when we shall see him, there is no beauty that we should desire him. He is despised and rejected of men; a man of sorrows, and acquainted with grief: and we hid as it were our faces from him; he was despised, and we esteemed him not." Many passages might be cited from the other prophets, but these are enough to justify the assertion made by St Paul to the Jews of Antioch,— "Men and brethren, children of the stock of Abraham, and whosoever among you feareth God, to you is the word of this salvation sent. For they that dwell at Jerusalem, and their rulers, because they knew him not, nor yet the voices of the prophets which are read every Sabbath day, they have fulfilled them in condemning him."

Thus we find it clearly foretold that the Messiah was to be rejected by the Jewish nation.

FINAL RESTORATION OF THE JEWS. 139

This rejection was necessary to the accomplishing of the purpose for which He came into the world. He came, not, as they imagined, to erect a temporal kingdom, but to make an atonement for human guilt, which could only be done by His voluntary humiliation and sufferings. His being treated by His own countrymen as an impostor, and being given up by them to the Romans that He might be crucified, was therefore appointed by a divine decree which the Jews were the guilty and unconscious instruments of fulfilling.

The rejection of Jesus as the Messiah may be traced to the fact, that they overlooked those prophecies which described His humiliation and sufferings at His first advent, but confined their attention to those which foretold the future elevation of His kingdom above all temporal dominions. Hence they expected Him to come as a mighty conqueror, and would not receive Him in the guise of a humble Nazarene. Notwithstanding which, there were some who looked upon Jesus as the true Messiah, and were able to see through the shadows of the law to the substance; rejoiced in the hope of a spiritual Redeemer, and panted for an inheritance in the celestial Canaan.

Even these were not wholly free from the prejudices of their countrymen; but being influenced by a spirit of true piety, they were convinced by the miracles which Jesus wrought, and waited for the time when He should fully clear up the mist that obscured their prospect. These, when they embraced Christ, gradually became blended with the general mass of His followers; consequently, though their conversion gave at that time a strong attestation to His doctrine, it does not at this day afford so distinct and clear an evidence. Those, however, who expected a temporal conqueror rejected Him, and by that rejection, as we have seen, fulfilled the prophecies, and were the occasion of His death, by which the redemption of mankind was accomplished.

With respect to the rejection of the Jews, for a time, from being God's people, this also was clearly foretold by all their prophets, and was in like manner subservient to very important ends which God had from the beginning predetermined.

When Moses commanded them to hearken to that Prophet whom the Lord their God would raise up unto them like unto himself, he intimated that some would refuse to do so, and declared that the Lord would require it at their hands. With wonderful particularity he foretold the events of that fatal siege which ended in the destruction of their city and temple, and in the complete overthrow of their civil and ecclesiastical polity: he foretold also their rejection, and the admission of the Gentiles to their privileges. Let the 26th chapter of Leviticus, and the 28th and 32d of Deuteronomy be attentively studied, and it will be apparent that the calamities brought upon them by the Romans were foreseen from the beginning of their existence as a nation. Numberless other passages might be brought from the succeeding prophets, but that which was already referred to in the 9th chapter of Daniel may suffice. After declaring that "the Messiah shall be cut off, but not for himself," he adds: "And the people of the prince that shall come shall destroy the city and the sanctuary; and the end thereof shall be with a flood, and unto the end of the war desolations are determined." It is well known that Christ whilst upon earth delivered a most remarkable prophecy on the subject, and immediately described the most important circumstances and consequences of the siege. This prophecy exactly coincides with the narratives that Josephus and Tacitus have left us concerning it.

But this event was in another important respect conducive to the fulfilment of the divine purposes. It manifested, in the most convincing manner, the abrogation of the Mosaic ritual, which could no longer be observed after the temple was destroyed, and the priesthood and the nation dispersed throughout the earth. A full refutation was hereby given to the Jewish idea that this economy was to last for ever—a satisfactory proof was afforded that men were no longer to worship at Jerusalem, but that the true worshippers of God were from thenceforth everywhere to pay their adoration to Him in spirit and in truth. The middle wall of partition had

FINAL RESTORATION OF THE JEWS. 143

indeed been broken down by the death of Christ, and by the call of the Gentiles into the Church, but now everything which contributed to encourage separation was removed, and believers both from among the Jews and Gentiles were gathered together, so as to form one fold under one Shepherd.

The real object of the Jewish economy was now clearly proclaimed. It was made manifest that the Jewish people had been separated to preserve the knowledge of the true God, and of the predictions concerning the Messiah, until He actually made His appearance. But when the glorious fabric of the Christian Church was completed, the legal dispensation which had served but as a scaffolding for the erection of it was taken down—the material temple was destroyed, and that spiritual temple erected which is to endure for ever. The Jews, however, have not ceased to be the witnesses of Christ, on account of their refusal to obey Him, and their consequent exclusion from His covenant. They bear indeed an unwilling testimony, but it is one which does not afford the less convincing evidence. Had the whole Jewish nation received the Messiah and agreed in acknowledging the truth of His religion, they would have become blended with the common mass of Christians, and we should by no means have possessed so satisfactory an attestation, as we now have, of the predictions concerning Him. Their sacred books would then have been far from affording that convincing evidence which they now yield, because it might have been alleged that they were forged, or at least interpolated, to gain credit for a belief with which some Jewish impostors had deceived their countrymen. But now that they reject Christianity, which derives its main support from the very books which they themselves acknowledge to have been given by divine inspiration, they afford an evidence to the truth of Christianity, the force of which no candid and reflecting mind can fail to perceive. It is plain that they would never have allowed their Scriptures to be interpolated in order to support the cause of Christianity, and it is no less evident from a comparison of those Scriptures with the doctrines and miracles of Jesus, that He was indeed that divine personage who had been foretold from the earliest ages as the Redeemer of lost mankind.

The preservation of the Jews as a distinct people, notwithstanding all the miseries and persecutions which they have for so many ages endured, is a remarkable manifestation of the hand of God.

Where is the conquered nation which has not sooner or later been mingled with their conquerors?

The Babylonian, the Persian, and the Macedonian empires having in turn destroyed each other, were all at length absorbed by the Roman. This mighty state itself at length became a prey to the Gothic and Vandalic hordes, and scarcely a descendant of its ancient families can now be found. But the Jews, though dispersed throughout the earth, are still preserved as a distinct people. Though, in conformity with the prediction of the text, they have been for nearly eighteen centuries without a king, without a prince, and without a sacrifice, or any kind of divine communication; though they have been, as Moses foretold they should be, a proverb and a byword amongst all the nations, and their land a desolation; still they exist, still they are numerous, still they retain a strong attachment to their ancient religion, still they cherish the hope that their long-looked-for Messiah will appear and restore their nation to happiness and glory.

Who that considers this subject with the attention which it deserves can help discovering the direction of Providence in everything which has befallen this wonderful people? It is manifest that they were chosen to be the guardians and almoners of "the oracles of God;" to preserve a light, which should shine in the midst of darkness, and which should not be extinguished till "the Sun of Righteousness" had risen upon the earth. Their deliverance from Egypt, their establishment in Canaan, their division into two kingdoms, their captivities and dispersions, all tended to attract the attention of other nations to those truths which, though originally revealed to all men, had been corrupted and obscured by every people but themselves. The mixture of temporal with spiritual promises in their law served to make them cherish it with more scrupulous exactness, and afforded a powerful motive to those amongst them who would have been but faintly influenced by the hope of a future and heavenly felicity. And when at length, according to the plan of Providence, they were driven from the land of Canaan, they carried into every region the authentic copies of their Scriptures; and so anxiously scrupulous were they to preserve the purity of the text of the Old Testament, which they saved from the wreck of their nationality, that their learned doctors counted every book, every chapter, every verse, every word, every letter in the Bible, and how often each letter of the alphabet occurs in it; and to this day you will find at the end of each book in the Hebrew Bible, the number of chapters, verses, words, &c. &c., contained in it. Thus they bear an unsuspected witness to the truths of Christianity, which they themselves blindly reject. That they should continue a distinct people was as plainly foretold as that they should be scattered throughout every nation under heaven; for God, we are assured, has glorious designs concerning them. He has said:—"Fear thou not, O Jacob my servant, for I am with thee, for I will make a full end of all the nations whither I have driven thee: but I will not make a full end of thee." He has declared that though "the children of Israel shall abide many days without a king, and without a prince, and without a sacrifice, and without an image, and without an ephod, and without teraphim;" yet, "afterwards shall the children of Israel return and seek the Lord their God, and David their king, and shall fear the Lord and his goodness in the latter days." We have seen in how remarkable a manner the former part of this prediction has been, and to this day continues to be, fulfilled: the latter part of it suggests reflections which must be reserved for the ensuing discourse. In it I shall endeavour to show that the Jews are destined to bear a still more signal testimony to the faith of Christ, when, through divine grace and mercy, they shall have been converted, and brought to acknowledge Jesus as their Messiah.

And now unto God and our Father be glory for ever and ever. Amen.

VIII.

THE CONVERSION AND FINAL RESTORATION OF THE JEWS—*continued*.

HOSEA iii. 5.

"Afterward shall the children of Israel return, and seek the Lord their God, and David their king; and shall fear the Lord and his goodness in the latter days."

IN my last discourse I took occasion from the preceding verse to consider the destruction of the Jewish polity, and the dispersion of the nation in consequence of their rejecting the Messiah, as well as the evidence which their present condition bears to the truth of revelation.

The more we reflect upon the subject, the more convinced must we be that the prophet could not have known these things if they had not been communicated to him by divine inspiration.

When he beheld Israel's sinful condition, he might, indeed, have concluded that they would draw down upon themselves heavy judgments: but to foresee that, though dispersed and distressed, they should still continue a separate people—a people without prince or ruler; that they should for so long a period neither have the power of offering sacrifices to Jehovah, nor the inclination to worship an idol; that their divinely-instituted ritual should be abrogated, and their self-invented superstitions be completely laid aside;—to foresee these things, I say, manifestly exceeded the utmost stretch of human foresight, and would have been impossible for any person who had not the Holy Spirit for his teacher.

To pretend that such a prophecy as this was written after the event would be in the highest degree absurd. For, independently of the evidence, both internal and external, that might be produced to show that Hosea wrote before the captivity of the ten tribes, the event itself is one which has taken ages to accomplish; it is one of which *we* at this day are witnesses, for the children of Israel even now continue "without a king, and without a prince, and without a sacrifice, and without an image, and without an ephod, and without teraphim." The words of the text, also, which are inseparably connected with the foregoing verse, relate to an event which has not yet been accomplished, but which we have the strongest reason to believe shall in due season be fulfilled.

Marvellous as have been the dealings of God with Israel, we are assured that yet more glorious things are in reserve for that highly-favoured nation. Unfaithful as she has proved herself to the covenant of her God, He has not cast her off for ever. Though He has given her a bill of divorcement, and has betrothed to himself a Church from amongst the Gentiles in her room, yet the strongest assurances have been made that He has mercy yet in store for her, and that she shall at the last be made sensible of the baseness of her infidelity, and be restored again to favour.

The metaphor which has been here adopted is suggested by the former part of this chapter, and harmonises with many other parts of Scripture.

The Jewish nation have during their dispersion entirely abstained from idolatry. Prone as they were to it, they have kept themselves perfectly free from it, and we cannot doubt, therefore, that the mercy promised to them shall be displayed in its full extent. The prophecies which relate to this subject are so numerous that, were they all to be selected and commented on, they would fill a volume of no inconsiderable magnitude. I will therefore content myself with citing some which speak of the restoration and conversion of Israel; of the destruction of their enemies, and of the conversion of the Gentile nations in consequence of the marvellous works which God will perform in their behalf.

So wonderfully is *mercy* mingled with *judgment* in the divine dealings, that almost all the prophecies which have been delivered concerning their *unbelief* and its *punishment*, foretells also their *restoration* and *conversion*.

God had promised Abraham, "I will establish

my covenant between me and thee, and thy seed after thee, in their generations, for an everlasting covenant, to be a God unto thee, and to thy seed after thee. And I will give unto thee, and to thy seed after thee, the land wherein thou art a stranger, all the land of Canaan, for an everlasting possession; and I will be their God," (Gen. xvii. 7, 8.)

To this covenant we find a continual reference. After describing the calamities which would come upon them, God continues thus to speak: —"And yet for all that, when they be in the land of their enemies, I will not cast them away, neither will I abhor them, to destroy them utterly, and to break my covenant with them: for I am the Lord their God. But I will for their sakes remember the covenant of their ancestors, whom I brought forth out of the land of Egypt, in the sight of the heathen, that I might be their God," (Lev. xxvi. 44, 45.)

A similar promise is given in the 30th chapter of Deuteronomy, that they shall repent and be converted, and it is said that "then the Lord thy God will turn thy captivity, and have compassion upon thee, and will return and gather thee from all the nations, whither the Lord thy God hath scattered thee. If any of thine be driven out unto the outmost parts of heaven, from thence will the Lord thy God gather thee, and from thence will he fetch thee: and the Lord thy God will bring thee into the land which thy fathers possessed, and thou shalt possess it; and he will do thee good, and multiply thee above thy fathers.* And the Lord thy God will circumcise thine heart, and the heart of thy seed, to love the Lord thy God with all thine heart, and with all thy soul, that thou mayest live." In Deut. xxxii. 36, it is also said: —" The Lord shall judge his people, and repent himself for his servants, when he seeth that their power is gone, and there is none shut up, or left."

In the psalm which David appointed to be sung when the ark was brought to Mount Zion, he reminded the people of this covenant, and insisted on its perpetuity:—"Be ye mindful always

---

* Witsius justly observes that this was not accomplished in the return from the Babylonish captivity, and therefore remains yet to be fulfilled.

of his covenant ; the word which he commanded to a thousand generations ; even of the covenant which he made with Abraham, and of his oath unto Isaac; and hath confirmed the same to Jacob for a law, and to Israel for an everlasting covenant, saying, Unto thee will I give the land of Canaan, the lot of your inheritance," (1 Chron. xvi. 15-18.)

The prophet Isaiah, after giving a most beautiful description of the blessings of Christ's kingdom, adds:—"It shall come to pass in that day, that the Lord shall set his hand again the *second* time to recover the remnant of his people, which shall be left, from Assyria, and from Egypt, and from Pathros, and from Cush, and from Elam, and from Shinar, and from Hamath, and from the islands of the sea. And he shall set up an ensign for the nations, and shall assemble the outcasts of Israel, and gather together the dispersed of Judah from the four corners of the earth. The envy also of Ephraim shall depart, and the adversaries of Judah shall be cut off: Ephraim shall not envy Judah, and Judah shall not vex Ephraim," (chap. xi. 11–13.)

He describes the same events in other places: —"The ransomed of the Lord shall return, and come to Zion with songs and everlasting joy upon their heads: they shall obtain joy and gladness, and sorrow and sighing shall flee away," (chap. xxxv. 10.) "I will bring the blind by a way that they knew not; I will lead them in paths that they have not known: I will make darkness light before them, and crooked things straight. These things will I do unto them, and not forsake them," (chap. xlii. 16.) "Thus saith the Lord that created thee, O Jacob, and he that formed thee, O Israel, Fear not: for I have redeemed thee, I have called thee by thy name; thou art mine. . . . . Fear not: for I am with thee: I will bring thy seed from the east, and gather thee from the west; I will say to the north, Give up; and to the south, Keep not back: bring my sons from far, and my daughters from the ends of the earth; even every one that is called by my name: for I have created him for my glory, I have formed him; yea, I have made him," (chap. xliii. 1. 5–7.) "Look unto me, and be ye saved, all the ends of the earth: for I am God, and there is none else. I have sworn by myself, the word is gone out of my mouth in righteousness, and shall not return, That unto me every knee shall bow, every tongue shall swear. Surely, shall one say, in the Lord have I righteousness and strength: even to him shall men come; and all that are incensed against him shall be ashamed. In the Lord shall all the seed of Israel be justified, and shall glory," (chap. xlv. 22–25.) "Thus saith the Lord, In an acceptable time have I heard thee, and in a day of salvation have I helped thee: and I will preserve thee, and give thee for a covenant of the people, to establish the earth, to cause to inherit the desolate heritages; that thou mayest say to the prisoners, Go forth; to them that are in darkness, Show yourselves. They shall feed in the ways, and their pastures shall be in all high places. They shall not hunger nor thirst; neither shall the heat nor sun smite them: for he that hath mercy on them shall lead them, even by the springs of water shall he guide them. And I will make all my mountains a way, and my highways shall be exalted. Behold, these shall come from far: and, lo, these from the north and from the west; and these from the land of Sinim. Sing, O heavens; and be joyful, O earth; and break forth into singing, O mountains: for the Lord hath comforted his people, and will have mercy upon his afflicted. . . . . Thus saith the Lord God, Behold, I will lift up mine hand to the Gentiles, and set up my standard to the people: and they shall bring thy sons in their arms, and thy daughters shall be carried upon their shoulders. And kings shall be thy nursing fathers, and their queens thy nursing mothers: they shall bow down to thee with their face toward the earth, and lick up the dust of thy feet; and thou shalt know that I am the Lord: for they shall not be ashamed that wait for me," (chap. xlix. 8-13, 22, 23.) "Awake, awake; put on thy strength, O Zion; put on thy beautiful garments, O Jerusalem, the holy city: for henceforth there shall no more come into thee the uncircumcised and the unclean. Shake thyself from the dust; arise, and sit down, O Jerusalem: loose thyself from the bands of thy neck, O captive daughter of Zion.

For thus saith the Lord, Ye have sold yourselves for nought; and ye shall be redeemed without money," (chap. lii. 1–3.) "O thou afflicted, tossed with tempest, and not comforted, behold, I will lay thy stones with fair colours, and lay thy foundations with sapphires. And I will make thy windows of agates, and thy gates of carbuncles, and all thy borders of pleasant stones. And all thy children shall be taught of the Lord; and great shall be the peace of thy children. In righteousness shalt thou be established: thou shalt be far from oppression; for thou shalt not fear: and from terror; for it shall not come near thee," (chap. liv. 11–14.) "Arise, shine; for thy light is come, and the glory of the Lord is risen upon thee. For, behold, the darkness shall cover the earth, and gross darkness the people: but the Lord shall arise upon thee, and his glory shall be seen upon thee. And the Gentiles shall come to thy light, and kings to the brightness of thy rising. Lift up thine eyes round about, and see: all they gather themselves together, they come to thee: thy sons shall come from far, and thy daughters shall be nursed at thy side. . . . .

Whereas thou hast been forsaken and hated, so that no man went through thee, I will make thee an eternal excellency, a joy of many generations. Thou shalt also suck the milk of the Gentiles, and shalt suck the breast of kings: and thou shalt know that I the Lord am thy Saviour and thy Redeemer, the mighty One of Jacob. For brass I will bring gold, and for iron I will bring silver, and for wood brass, and for stones iron: I will also make thy officers peace, and thine exactors righteousness. Violence shall no more be heard in thy land, wasting nor destruction within thy borders; but thou shalt call thy walls Salvation, and thy gates Praise. The sun shall be no more thy light by day; neither for brightness shall the moon give light unto thee: but the Lord shall be unto thee an everlasting light, and thy God thy glory. . . . . Thy people also shall be all righteous: they shall inherit the land for ever, the branch of my planting, the work of my hands, that I may be glorified. A little one shall become a thousand, and a small one a strong nation: I the Lord will hasten it in his time," (chap. lx. 1–4; 15–22.) " Behold, the Lord

L

hath proclaimed unto the end of the world, Say ye to the daughter of Zion, Behold, thy salvation cometh; behold, his reward is with him, and his work before him. And they shall call them, The holy people, The redeemed of the Lord; and thou shalt be called, *Sought out, A city not forsaken,*" (chap. lxii. 11, 12.)

In this beautiful manner does the prophet Isaiah describe the restoration and conversion of the Jewish nation. Many of these passages, as well as others which have been unavoidably passed by, have been erroneously applied to the success of the gospel when first preached, and to the selection of a church from amongst the Gentiles; whereas, taken according to their natural sense, and that which best harmonises with the context as well as with the parallel parts of Scripture, they describe events of the most glorious nature which yet remain to be fulfilled. Predictions of the same kind abound in the writings of the other prophets. In Jeremiah xxiii. 2-6, we read:—"Thus saith the Lord God of Israel, ... I will gather the remnant of my flock out of all countries whither

I have driven them, and will bring them again to their folds; and they shall be fruitful and increase. And I will set up shepherds over them, which shall feed them; and they shall fear no more, nor be dismayed, neither shall they be lacking, saith the Lord. Behold, the days come, saith the Lord, that I will raise unto David a righteous Branch, and a King shall reign and prosper, and shall execute judgment and justice in the earth. In his days Judah shall be saved, and Israel shall dwell safely; and this is his name whereby he shall be called, The Lord our Righteousness." Again, we read in chap. xxx. 10, 11 :—" Fear thou not, O my servant Jacob, saith the Lord; neither be dismayed, O Israel; for, lo, I will save thee from afar, and thy seed from the land of their captivity; and Jacob shall return, and shall be in rest, and be quiet, and none shall make him afraid. For I am with thee, saith the Lord, to save thee: though I make a full end of all nations whither I have scattered thee, yet will I not make a full end of thee; but I will correct thee in measure, and will not leave thee altogether unpunished." It is also written in chap. xxxi. 7-11, 31-34—"Thus saith the Lord, Sing with gladness for Jacob, and shout among the chief of the nations: publish ye, praise ye, and say, O Lord, save thy people, the remnant of Israel. Behold, I will bring them from the north country, and gather them from the coasts of the earth, and with them the blind and the lame, the woman with child and her that travaileth with child together: a great company shall return thither. They shall come with weeping, and with supplications will I lead them: I will cause them to walk by the rivers of waters in a straight way, wherein they shall not stumble; for I am a father to Israel, and Ephraim is my first-born. Hear the word of the Lord, O ye nations, and declare it in the isles afar off, and say, He that scattered Israel will gather him, and keep him, as a shepherd doth his flock. For the Lord hath redeemed Jacob, and ransomed him from the hand of him that was stronger than he. .... Behold, the days come, saith the Lord, that I will make a new covenant with the house of Israel, and with the house of Judah; not according to the covenant that I made with their fathers in the day that I took them by the hand to bring them out of the land of Egypt, (which my covenant they brake, although I was an husband unto them, saith the Lord;) but this shall be the covenant that I will make with the house of Israel; After those days, saith the Lord, I will put my law in their inward parts, and write it in their hearts; and will be their God, and they shall be my people. And they shall teach no more every man his neighbour, and every man his brother, saying, Know the Lord: for they shall all know me, from the least of them unto the greatest of them, saith the Lord: for I will forgive their iniquity, and I will remember their sin no more."

The prophet Ezekiel describes a very remarkable vision which was vouchsafed to him, and which has an evident relation to this subject. He saw a large valley filled with dry bones, which, at the command of the Lord, were covered with sinews and with flesh, and animated with life by His Spirit. This resurrection of the bones is declared to be typical of the restoration of Israel. "Then he said unto me, Son of man, these bones are the whole house of Israel: behold, they say, Our bones are dried, and our hope is lost; we are cut off for our parts. Therefore prophesy and say unto them, Thus saith the Lord God, Behold, O my people, I will open your graves, and cause you to come up out of your graves, and bring you into the land of Israel. And ye shall know that I am the Lord, when I have opened your graves, O my people, and brought you up out of your graves, and shall put my Spirit in you, and ye shall live, and I shall place you in your own land: then shall ye know that I the Lord have spoken it, and performed it, saith the Lord," (Ezek. xxxvii. 11-14.)

Another emblem is also recorded in the same chapter. It is the miraculous union of two sticks, on which the names of Judah and his companions, and of Joseph and his companions, had respectively been written. This emblem is thus explained:—"Thus saith the Lord God,

Behold, I will take the children of Israel from among the heathen, whither they be gone, and will gather them on every side, and bring them into their own land: and I will make them one nation in the land upon the mountains of Israel; and one king shall be king to them all: and they shall be no more two nations, neither shall they be divided into two kingdoms any more at all: neither shall they defile themselves any more with their idols, nor with their detestable things, nor with any of their transgressions: but I will save them out of all their dwelling-places, wherein they have sinned, and will cleanse them; so shall they be my people, and I will be their God. And David my servant shall be king over them; and they all shall have one shepherd: they shall also walk in my judgments, and observe my statutes, and do them. And they shall dwell in the land that I have given unto Jacob my servant, wherein your fathers have dwelt; and they shall dwell therein, even they, and their children, and their children's children, for ever; and my servant David shall be their prince for ever," (Ezek. xxxvii. 21-25.)

The conversion of the Jewish nation to the faith of Christ is spoken of so distinctly by the prophet Zechariah, that it seems truly astonishing that they can shut their eyes to the evidence which it affords. In Zech. xii. 10, the Lord speaks thus :—" I will pour upon the house of David, and upon the inhabitants of Jerusalem, the spirit of grace and of supplications; and they shall look upon me whom they have pierced, and they shall mourn for him, as one mourneth for his only son, and shall be in bitterness for him, as one that is in bitterness for his first-born."

That this promise does not, when taken in its fullest extent, relate to the conversion of those Jews who were pricked at heart by the preaching of Peter on the day of Pentecost, will be evident to those who consider the context, in which it is coupled with that of the destruction of the enemies of Judah, and the complete re-establishment of the nation at Jerusalem. But, of all the prophecies which have been left us concerning the conversion of Israel, that of St Paul, in Rom. xi. 25-27, is the most satisfactory :— " I would not, brethren, that ye should be ignorant of this mystery, (lest ye should be wise in your own conceits,) that blindness in part is happened to Israel, until the fulness of the Gentiles be come in. And so all Israel shall be saved; as it is written, There shall come out of Sion the Deliverer, and shall turn away ungodliness from Jacob: for this is my covenant unto them, when I shall take away their sins."

These passages of Scripture, with many others to the same effect, appear decisively to prove that a period is fixed in the counsels of Jehovah when the dispersion of Israel shall be at an end, and when they shall once more be restored to the land of their inheritance. They shall be gathered together from all the nations through which they have been scattered, and miracles, even yet more signal than those which attended their deliverance from Egypt, shall be performed in their behalf, so that they shall not "remember the former things, neither consider the things of old."

The destruction of those who shall oppose

their return and re-establishment is foretold in no less emphatic language. After predicting these events in a passage which has been already quoted, Isaiah thus continues, (chap. xlix. 25, 26):—" Thus saith the Lord, Even the captives of the mighty shall be taken away, and the prey of the terrible shall be delivered : for I will contend with him that contendeth with thee, and I will save thy children. And I will feed them that oppress thee with their own flesh ; and they shall be drunken with their own blood, as with sweet wine ; and all flesh shall know that I the Lord am thy Saviour and thy Redeemer, the mighty One of Jacob." Again, in chap. lix. 19, 20 :— " They shall fear the name of the Lord from the west, and his glory from the rising of the sun. When the enemy shall come in like a flood, the Spirit of the Lord shall lift up a standard against him. And the Redeemer shall come to Zion, and unto them that turn from transgression in Jacob, saith the Lord." Also in chap. lxiii. 1-4: —" Who is this that cometh from Edom, with dyed garments from Bozrah ? this that is glorious in his apparel, travelling in the greatness of his strength? I that speak in righteousness, mighty to save. Wherefore art thou red in thine apparel, and thy garments like him that treadeth in the winefat? I have trodden the winepress alone; and of the people there was none with me: for I will tread them in mine anger, and trample them in my fury; and their blood shall be sprinkled upon my garments, and I will stain all my raiment. For the day of vengeance is in mine heart, and the year of my redeemed is come."

In Joel iii. 1, 2, 16, 17, it is thus written:—" Behold, in those days, and in that time, when I shall bring again the captivity of Judah and Jerusalem, I will also gather all nations, and will bring them down into the valley of Jehoshaphat, and will plead with them there for my people and for my heritage Israel, whom they have scattered among the nations, and parted my land. . . . . The Lord shall roar out of Zion, and utter his voice from Jerusalem; and the heavens and the earth shall shake: but the Lord will be the hope of his people, and the strength of the children of Israel. So shall ye know that I am the Lord your God dwelling in Zion, my holy mountain : then shall Jerusalem be holy, and there shall no strangers pass through her any more."

In Zeph. iii. 8 it is also said :—" Wait ye upon me, saith the Lord, until the day that I rise up to the prey : for my determination is to gather the nations, that I may assemble the kingdoms, to pour upon them mine indignation, even all my fierce anger : for all the earth shall be devoured with the fire of my jealousy." And again, in Zech. xii. 6, 8 :—" In that day will I make the governors of Judah like an hearth of fire among the wood, and like a torch of fire in a sheaf; and they shall devour all the people round about, on the right hand and on the left : and Jerusalem shall be inhabited again in her own place, even in Jerusalem. . . . . In that day shall the Lord defend the inhabitants of Jerusalem ; and he that is feeble among them at that day shall be as David ; and the house of David shall be as God, as the angel of the Lord before them."

Thus shall this long dispersed and persecuted

people be delivered from all their adversaries. The arm of the Most High shall be made bare for their defence. He will bring to naught every counsel and break up every confederacy which shall be formed against them. Their enemies shall be smitten with a miraculous and fearful destruction, but they shall be established in peace and prosperity under the government of their long-expected Messiah, whom they shall acknowledge with mingled joy and lamentation, confessing their sin in rejecting Him, and worshipping Him now with the most fervent adoration. No longer shall they wish to see the knowledge of the Messiah restricted to their own nation, but shall rejoice to become instrumental in spreading the glad tidings of salvation amongst those who yet remain unacquainted with the saving truths of the gospel. That the Jews when brought to the knowledge of Christ, shall be instrumental in diffusing it, is clearly foretold by the prophets; and when we consider their miraculous preservation to this day amongst all the nations of the earth, and consequent acquaintance with all the languages of the different people amongst whom they reside, we may readily conclude that no other missionaries can be so fully qualified for the purpose.

Isaiah, in his second chapter, (ver. 2, 3,) says :—." It shall come to pass in the last days, that the mountain of the Lord's house shall be established in the top of the mountains, and shall be exalted above the hills ; and all nations shall flow unto it. And many people shall go and say, Come ye, and let us go up to the mountain of the Lord, to the house of the God of Jacob ; and he will teach us of his ways, and we will walk in his paths : for out of Zion shall go forth the law, and the word of the Lord from Jerusalem." Also in chap. lxi. 6 : "Ye shall be named the Priests of the Lord : men shall call you the ministers of our God : ye shall eat the riches of the Gentiles, and in their glory shall ye boast yourselves." And in chap. lxvi. 21-23 : "I will also take of them for priests, and for Levites, saith the Lord. For as the new heavens, and the new earth, which I will make, shall remain before me, saith the Lord, so shall your seed and your name remain. And it shall come to pass, that from one new moon to another, and from one sabbath to another, shall all flesh come to worship before me, saith the Lord." The other prophets lead us to entertain similar expectations. Thus Zephaniah, in chap. iii. 9, 10, "Then will I turn to the people a pure language, that they may all call upon the name of the Lord, to serve him with one consent. From beyond the rivers of Ethiopia my suppliants, even the daughter of my dispersed, shall bring mine offering." Zechariah writes thus, (chap. viii. 20–23) :—" Thus saith the Lord of hosts, It shall yet come to pass, that there shall come people, and the inhabitants of many cities: and the inhabitants of one city shall go to another, saying, Let us go speedily to pray before the Lord, and to seek the Lord of hosts: I will go also. Yea, many people and strong nations shall come to seek the Lord of hosts in Jerusalem, and to pray before the Lord. Thus saith the Lord of hosts, In those days it shall come to pass, that ten men shall take hold out of all languages of the nations, even *shall take hold of the skirt of him that is a Jew, saying, We will go with you: for we have heard that*

God is with you." Thus in its fullest extent shall be accomplished that prediction of the prophet Malachi (chap. i. 11):—"From the rising of the sun even unto the going down of the same, my name shall be great among the Gentiles; and in every place incense shall be offered unto my name, and a pure offering; for my name shall be great among the heathen, saith the Lord of hosts."

Glorious, indeed, are the predictions which we have been reviewing. They relate to that dispensation to which all that we had before considered is subordinate—that dispensation which shall extend the empire of Christ over every climate and region of the globe. It is now a little more than sixty years since the modern missionary movement commenced, and although the efforts amongst Jews and Gentiles have been crowned with God's blessing, little has been accomplished in comparison with what remains yet to be achieved. If we consult the oracles of God, how cheering the description of the ultimate triumphs of the gospel! How bright the missionary pictures!—"The kingdoms of this world

FINAL RESTORATION OF THE JEWS. 177

shall become the kingdoms of our Lord and of his Christ." "At the name of Jesus every knee should bow, of things in heaven, and things in earth, and things under the earth; and that every tongue should confess that Jesus Christ is Lord, to the glory of God the Father." "The earth shall be filled with the knowledge of the Lord, as the waters cover the sea," &c. &c.

How painful is the contrast between what the world *is*, and what it is *to be!*

According to a late estimate, the world contains a population of about twelve hundred millions. Of this nearly nine hundred millions are Pagans, Mohammedans, and Jews—of the latter about ten millions. The remaining three hundred millions constitute Christendom. Of this nearly two hundred millions are Romanists, while some fifty millions belong to the Greek Church; the rest consist of Protestants, many of whom, alas! it is feared, have the form of godliness, but are strangers to the power of it. Is this not a truly appalling picture to behold, and that in the nineteenth century of the Christian era? We trace with painful emotion the present condition of the world—several hundred millions of human beings still living in heathen ignorance! Nearly two hundred millions blindly adhering to the superstitious and idolatrous system of Rome. One hundred millions deluded by the Arabian impostor, while many who call themselves Protestants, and even fill places of high position within the Church, are not only destitute of vital godliness, but are actually undermining our Zion.

Whilst we grieve to reflect on this state of things, we at the same time acknowledge that all this was foreseen and permitted by Infinite Wisdom, and, we may be assured, for the wisest purposes. Though the patience and faith of the saints have been severely tried—though the witnesses of Christ have prophesied in sackcloth—they have still not ceased to prophesy; the lamp of the sanctuary has not been wholly extinguished; the servants of the Lamb have not been completely extirpated.

Already has the apocalyptic angel fled through the midst of heaven, declaring the everlasting gospel which shall assuredly be made known unto them that dwell on the earth, to every nation, and kindred, and tongue, and people. The fall of the mystic Babylon is evidently near at hand, notwithstanding her *apparent* inroads upon the Church of God.

We may reasonably expect that the times of the Gentiles are nearly fulfilled, and that the period during which the Holy City is to be trodden under foot is almost expired. We have the authority of Daniel for believing that when the Mohammedan imposture and the Papal domination have lasted twelve hundred and sixty years, they shall be destroyed, and the restoration of the Jews shall commence. That the greater part of those years must have elapsed is notorious to all who are acquainted with modern history. That the revolutions which have taken place within the present century in Europe, and the importance and high positions which the Jews have obtained, and now hold, throughout the world, we may say, certainly favour the supposition of their national restoration to the Holy Land. With humble hope we may look forward to the perfect completion of all those predictions and promises which have passed in review before us in the present discourse. Presumptuous, indeed, would it be to assert that these things will take place in this generation, or to attempt to fix the times and the seasons which the Father has put into His own power; but of this we may be fully assured, that He will fulfil all His promises, and bring to pass all things which He hath spoken by the mouth of His holy prophets, which have been since the world began.

Let us now pause, and take a brief retrospective view of the ground over which we have travelled. We have seen the great Creator of the universe calling this world out of nothing, and placing man upon it in a state of probation. Scarcely are the first human beings created, before we see them revolting from their heavenly Sovereign, and entailing guilt and misery on themselves and on their posterity. We trace the fatal consequences of their crime in the prevalence of universal depravity. At the same time we trace the promise of a Redeemer given immediately after the fall, and confirmed by repeated disclosures. We perceive manifestations of the power and grace of the Holy Spirit, in the preservation of a succession of faithful and holy men amidst the general corruption of the human race. At one time the Church is confined to the single family of Noah, and is shortly after restricted to that of one of his children. Almost expiring, it is revived in Abraham and in his descendants. We then witness the establishment of a new economy. We find an ecclesiastical polity regularly formed; a tabernacle erected in which the divine presence is gloriously displayed; a peculiar mode of worship instituted of such a nature as at once to secure the Israelites from the contagion of idolatry, and to make them instruments for preserving the knowledge of the true God for the benefit of all nations.

Though at first in a great measure detached from the rest of the world, yet, in the course of time—by commerce, by alliance, and even by captivity amongst them—they were made instrumental to extend the light of revelation amongst the principal nations of the heathen world,—in such a degree, at least, as to prepare them for the appearance of the Messiah. When He came, indeed, we saw the greater part of them rejecting those credentials which so strongly authenticated His divine mission, and, in consequence, being themselves rejected from the distinguished place which they held in the divine favour. Yet even in this state of degradation, dispersed and despised as they have been, they have borne a most convincing, though unintentional, witness to the truth of God.

They have realised those prophecies which had so many ages before been delivered concerning them, as well as borne an unsuspected witness to those sacred writings which so clearly point out the Messiah. Preserved thus wonderfully, and under circumstances which could not have failed, without the signal interposition of Providence, to destroy them from being a nation, we are assured that they shall yet be gathered together from every quarter of the globe, shall be reinstated in the land of their fathers, and be converted to the faith of their Redeemer. The exact accomplishment, even to the present time, of the predictions which have been delivered concerning them,—their national identity and their present condition, are powerful indications that all things which have been written in the Scriptures have been written by the inspiration of God.

For how can we contemplate so wonderful a series of events—a series beginning with the creation, continued without interruption to the present moment, and extending to the consummation of all things—without acknowledging that it was arranged in the divine counsels before the world began, and that infinite wisdom, power, and goodness are carrying on the glorious design to its full consummation?

I appeal now to every candid individual whether, when he contemplates the uniform plan which pervades the whole of the Bible—when he considers the testimony which in various ways has been borne throughout all ages by the Church of God—he can regard the Scriptures, or any portion of it, as a fabrication of human artifice? What though to us some parts of it may appear dark and hard to be understood, we may discover abundant reason to conclude that those which respect past times were clear to the ages to which they related, and that those which respect the future shall in due season be unveiled in perfect brightness.. Let none of us, then, allow our eyes to be closed, nor our hearts to be hardened by unbelief, but let us receive the witness which God has given us of His Son—a witness which, though obscurely intimated in the earliest ages, has ever since increased in brightness, and now beams forth in meridian splendour.

Addressing you, my brethren, who profess to believe the gospel, I would urge you not to receive the grace of God in vain. Surely so glorious a revelation was not vouchsafed to us that we should simply admire it, but that we should with meekness receive the ingrafted word, which is able to save the soul. Let us, then, more prayerfully study God's Word, which is able to make wise unto salvation, and which is as wise as any one need be. Let us remember the rich inheritance which Christ has purchased for us with His own precious blood, and unto which we are called. Let us press forward for the prize of our high calling of God in Christ Jesus, and tread in the footsteps of that blessed Redeemer. Let us fervently pray that the Spirit of grace may be poured upon Israel, and that the kingdom of Christ may come and comprehend within its wide dominion both Jew and Gentile, so that we may all become one fold under one Shepherd.

And now to God the Father, God the Son, and God the Holy Ghost, let us ascribe, as is most justly due, all glory and majesty, dominion and power, both now and ever. Amen.

Ballantyne, Roberts, & Company, Printers, Edinburgh.

www.ingramcontent.com/pod-product-compliance
Lightning Source LLC
Chambersburg PA
CBHW020847160426
43192CB00007B/819